S0-BCP-920

THE PERFECT WILL
OF GOD

THE
PERFECT WILL
OF GOD

A helpful handbook for saints who
are seeking that "perfect will
of God"

by
G. CHRISTIAN WEISS

MOODY PRESS
CHICAGO

© 1950 by
The Moody Bible Institute
of Chicago

ISBN: 0-8024-6468-8

Printed in the United States of America

CONTENTS

FOREWORD

IT HAS BEEN A PLEASURE to read the manuscript on "The Perfect Will of God," by our friend and brother in Christ, Rev. G. Christian Weiss, and it is a privilege to write a foreword to so helpful a treatise upon so vital a theme.

Mr. Weiss has written earnestly and clearly. There is no guesswork here, nor are there any strange and fanatical utterances. He has developed his theme constructively and intelligently. His points are scripturally treated and effectively emphasized. Much is said in few words, yet with sufficient elucidation to drive home the teaching expounded. The chapters are helpfully divided, and the references and quotations from the Scriptures are numerous and fitting.

Since this is not a review of the treatise, but simply a foreword to it, we must forbear in pointing out the salient points of teaching which a review would demand. We would like to say, however, that in discussing this very important theme, Mr. Weiss repeatedly calls attention to truths which are almost altogether overlooked and neglected in these days of "watered down" preaching and teaching. He goes to the bottom of things, reaching the heart and the will, as well as instructing the mind.

We sincerely hope and pray that this excellent study will fall into the hands of literally thousands of young and old among God's people, for it deserves a wide reading. When prayfully read, it will bring conviction. It will bless individuals and, through them, the churches. There will be no end to its far-reaching effects. We recommend it heartily and pray God's blessing upon it.

—W. S. HOTTEL

1

GOD HAS A PLAN
FOR HIS CHILDREN'S LIVES

THE FIRST THING that must take place within the Christian's consciousness in relation to the all-important matter of God's will, is to realize that God has a very definite plan and purpose for every redeemed life. The Christian's life is not like a bit of fuzz from a frozen pussy willow, tossed hither and yon through the atmosphere at the whim of the autumn breeze. There is a course and goal for each believer's life, marked out and set by a tender and wise Hand of a loving, heavenly Father.

Once this vital fact grips the heart and consciousness, the whole matter of living the Christian life takes on new meaning. To many this comes as a climactic and revolutionary experience. When once this great truth becomes a *conviction,* the logical result in the heart of every true child of God will be to *find out* what that will and plan for *his life* is. It is as this precious truth becomes a reality to him, and only as it does, that any Christian will get down to serious business seeking *that perfect will of God.* There can be little enthusiasm in one's seeking something one is not sure actually exists. Rest assured, Christian, a divine plan does exist for you—and rest not till you have sought and found that plan for your life.

The fact that God has a definite will and plan for each believer's life is abundantly proved. Nature itself would attest it as well as the Bible. If God has such wondrous plans for His natural creation as is apparent on every hand surely His children, as human beings and the very crown of creation, and as His "new creation" in Christ Jesus, would receive no less consideration. To reorientate yourself in the wonders of God's creation, read such books as *The Secret of the Universe* by Nathan Wood, *God and You* by Arthur I. Brown, and *The Heavens Declare His Glory* by Nettie Sletten; also view if you have the opportunity, the film productions of the Moody Institute of Science *The God of Creation, The God of the Atom, The Voice of the Deep, Dust or Destiny.* (The last named of these is unusually fine.) In this same connection read such Scriptures as Psalm 8, Psalm 19:1-6, Job 38, 39, Isaiah 40:12-15, Isaiah 55:8-10. After acquainting oneself with the glories of the created universe with all its perfect design, plans and intricacies, which the Psalmist referred to as "the work of thy (God's) fingers," what Christian could fail to conclude that the God who has so deliberately made all this also has a holy will and plan for his life?

In the Word of God there is amassed evidence that there is a divine plan for each redeemed life. David prayed, *"Teach me to do thy will for thou art my God,"* Ps. 143:10. Paul exhorted Christians to *"present your bodies a living sacrifice . . . that ye may prove what is that good, and acceptable, and perfect will of God"*,

Rom. 12:1, 2. The same apostle in Eph. 5:17 says, *"Be ye not unwise, but understanding what the will of the Lord is."* In Col. 1:9 he declares, *"We . . . desire that ye might be filled with the knowledge of His will."* In Colossians 4:12 we read, *"That ye may stand perfect and complete in the will of God."* Peter says, *"For it is better if the will of God be so, that ye suffer for well doing than for evil doing,"* I Pet. 3:17. Hebrews 10:36: *"For ye* have need of patience that *after ye have done the will of God, ye might receive the promise"* (the reward). The saints at Caesarea, concerned over the fact that the Spirit-filled prophet Agabus had predicted suffering and imprisonment for Paul in Jerusalem, finally ceased trying to dissuade Paul from making the journey, saying, *"The will of the Lord be done",* Acts 21:14. We cannot overlook here the glorious promise in I John 2:17, *"And the world passeth away, and the lust (desires) thereof, but he that doeth the will of God abideth forever."*

There are also a great many *examples* in the Bible of lives chosen by God for specific tasks—*lives that were lived in the will of God.* In the New Testament we have pre-eminently the example of our own elder Brother, the Lord Jesus Christ, the "Son of Man" and "servant of Jehovah." His birth and entire life were exactly according to the definite plan and specific will of God. Back in eternity, as He offered Himself for the great ministry of the Incarnation and Atonement, He said to the Father, "Lo, I come to do thy will, O God" (Heb. 10:9). That will embraced His entire earthly sojourn. All through His life He spoke and wrought in accordance with that will; how often the gospeller commented on His words and deeds, "That the Scriptures (where the will of God and the plan of redemption were revealed) might be fulfilled." He Himself repeatedly made such statements as "I came down from heaven not to do mine own (fleshly) will, but the will of Him that sent me" (John 6:38); "My meat is to do the will of Him that sent me" (John 4:34) etc. In the Garden of Gethsemane He sweat blood agonizing in prayer over the ordeal of the cross which loomed up before Him, and cried out, "Not my will but thine be done!" (Luke 22:42).

But lest some fail to apply this example to their own lives, and say, "It was different with Christ—He was the Son of God and of course came into the world in accordance with a divine plan, but with us it may not be the same—we cannot make such a comparison," let us draw several examples from men of like passions as we are. Another great New Testament example of a life patterned after the divine will is that of the Apostle Paul. From the very moment he met His Saviour and was marvelously converted, the cry of his soul was, *"Lord, what wilt thou have me to do?"* (Acts 9:6). At the same time, over in the city of Damascus the Lord was dealing with the disciple, Ananias, who was to be the *human instrument* in this case through whom the divine will would be revealed to Saul of Tarsus. When Ananias objected, fearing Saul as the chiefest persecutor of the Church, God said, *"Go thy way: for he is a chosen vessel unto me to bear my name before Gentiles (heathen), and kings, and the children of Israel . . . I will shew him how great things he must suffer for my name's sake",* (Acts 9:15, 16). Here, at the time of this man's spiritual birth, the whole panorama of his future life is laid out in view. And his succeeding life was lived after the pattern thus laid out: he did bear the name of Christ to the Gentiles, becoming the first great Apostle to the Gentile world; he testified also before kings, Agrippa, Felix, Festus, Sergius Paulus, several other rulers, and at last even before the Emperor Caesar himself; he presented Christ to the people of Israel throughout the entire world where they dwelt. And he certainly suffered "great things for Christ's name's sake" as the account of his life in Scripture reveals—all according to the will and plan of God. It is interesting to note how his ministry to the heathen world began. The story is recorded in Acts, chapter 13. We read there, in verse 2 and 3, "As they ministered to the Lord, and fasted, the Holy Ghost said, *"Separate me Barnabas and Saul for the work whereunto I have called them.* And when they had fasted and prayed, and laid their hands on them, they sent them away." Thus was inaugurated a great life and work according to the will of God.

In the Old Testament one sees these demonstrative lives by the score. There is the patriarch Abraham, called to be the father of the chosen nation. Then consider Joseph's unusual career, noting the words he spoke to his brethren after the many eventful years of separation, "Ye thought evil against me: but *God meant it unto good, to bring to pass, as it is this day, to save much people alive"* (Gen. 50:20). Consider his whole life in the light of this revealing statement, and apply the principle to your own life. Moses stands out in bold relief as a man for whose life God had a great plan and purpose—also his successor, Joshua. Then contemplate the life of David, of Elijah, Isaiah, Daniel, John the Baptist—time fails us to refer to them all.

13

Even outside of the Sacred Record one can point to multitudes of demonstrations of this same thing. Consider Luther, Wesley, Carey, Livingstone, Taylor, Moffat, Paton, Judson. Read the biographies of these and other servants of the Lord for clearer evidence of the point in question.

Now, if God has demonstrated in such numbers of cases that He had a specific will for individual saints' lives, why should you doubt that He has just as definite a will and plan for you? *God has a will for every Christian's life,* as definite for one as for the other, and not only for the select few who are called to devote their lives and time to "full-time service." The fact is that all Christians have a "full-time service" to render to the Lord, i.e. their whole lives are to be in submission to His will from the moment of conversion to the hour of death.

Dr. William W. Orr, in his booklet on the will of God has said, "Don't think that God's plan includes only ministers, Christian leaders, missionaries, Sunday school teachers, and lay *workers.* Rather, God invites every Christian from the least to the greatest to be a co-partner with Him in the accomplishment of this great task (Matt. 28:18-20). God wants your help. You may have thought God worked only through specially called people. The truth is that God calls everyone. The Great Commission is to all Christians. You're a missionary the moment you become a Christian.

"Do not misunderstand me, however; I am not implying that every Christian ought to seek to be a minister, foreign missionary, or actively engaged in some full-time Christian service. It is not safe for you to be in China if God wants you to serve Him in America. Nor

14

is it right for you to endeavor to be a preacher if God wants you to be a Christian businessman. God must have His representatives as workers in all walks of life. And every Christian is needed whether he be a storekeeper, a student, a housewife, or a street sweeper. Do not be misled into a false differentiation by dividing those who are in full-time Christian service and those who are in full-time secular service. All are important, and God uses everyone. God calls a Christian doctor or a Christian school teacher just as definitely as He calls an evangelist."

Can you think of a father who has no will or plan for the life of his son? Can you imagine a mother who has no clear will or definite ambition for her daughter? Can you imagine a man who has no special desire or pattern in the one he chooses to be his wife? Can you conceive of a king or ruler who has no will or desire or law to govern the conduct of his people? A captain who has no plan for his soldiery? An employer who has no plan or pattern to guide the labor of his workers? A shepherd who has no object in view for his sheep? A vine that has no positive purpose in its branches? If so, then you may also think that God does not have a plan for your life, for every one of these symbols is used in the Bible to represent the relation the Christian bears to His Lord.

Know, therefore, Christian, that God has a will and plan for your life.

2

IT IS POSSIBLE TO MISS GOD'S WILL
AND PLAN

WHEN I WAS A STUDENT in Christian training, one of
my teachers startled our ears one morning in class by
saying, "I have lived most of my life on God's second
best." Following that remark, instead of devoting the
class period to the lesson for the day, he felt prompted
by the Spirit to tell us his story: God had manifestly
called him to be a missionary in his younger years. He
turned aside from this course, through marriage. He
had in fact practically given up Christian work and
begun a selfish business life as cashier in a bank, with
the primary purpose of setting up a nice home and
making money. The Spirit of God kept dealing with
him, but there was no yielding. A number of years
passed. Then one day there was a telephone call to the
bank. Their small child had toppled over in her high
chair and was dead. It took that bitter experience to
bring this Christian to the place of surrender. After he
spent a night alone with God on his knees, in tears and
agony, the surrender came. But it was too late now to
go to Africa; his disobedience of earlier years had

closed that door forever, though he knew God *had once called him.*

What was to be done in a case like that? Surrendering himself then and there utterly to God, with a broken and contrite heart, this man pleaded with the Lord to take up the tangled threads of his disobedient life and make of the wreckage whatever He could. God heard that prayer, and gave him a useful and quite fruitful ministry the rest of his days. He was the means eventually of training and helping to send out other missionaries. But, as he testified with tears to us young men that morning, he had missed God's first and highest choice for his life and had been living on His second best.

I have since met numerous people who have borne similar testimony. Usually these testimonies have been bathed, or at least marked, with bitter tears. For, while, thank God, He has ways of using even those who have sinned and have gone past that single entrance into the channel of His perfect will, life can never be the way He originally intended it. It is a tragedy to miss the perfect will of God for one's life. Christian, mark well these words and this testimony, lest you too miss His first choice. God doubtless will use any life that is submitted to His hands, anywhere along life's pathway, but let us be among those who have sought and surrendered to His will at the outset of life's journey, and thus avoid those painful and shameful detours of the way.

There are some sad cases in the Bible, too, of men who by-passed God's will. Saul, first king of the Hebrews, is an outstanding and sorrowful example. He was God's choice for the throne of Israel, and also the choice of the people (I Sam. 9:15-20; 10:1,6; 10:17-24). Everything was in his favor. He was divine-

17

ly called, annointed and publicly coronated to fill the role of leader, captain, and king of Israel. The Spirit of God came upon him for his task. But through selfish pride and insane jealousy Saul turned aside from the divine path of blessing (I Sam. 13:9-14; 15:13-26, 35; 28:7-9; 31:3-5). The Spirit of God departed from him, and he was rejected by God and another was chosen to carry out his task. His life ended in failure, disgrace, defeat, and finally, suicide.

Solomon too is a sobering example of the same tragic thing. Though he served long as a wise ruler in Israel in the pure will of God, he allowed the love of women and the lust of his flesh to lead him astray. Because of his disobedience and failure he was told that the kingdom would, after his decease, be divided and would disintegrate. It was only because of the promise the Lord had made with his father, David, in behalf of Solomon, that the disintegration did not take place during his lifetime. Many a man, like Solomon, though "wise" in many respects, has missed God's will for his life through love of women, or a woman. I refer particularly to those who ignore the known will of God for their lives and enter into marriage with a partner who never could, or would, go the direction of God's choice. Many a person who has surrendered everything else on God's altar, has been unwilling to surrender his love-life and has because of this made havoc of his whole life. Also one comes across sad examples of men who apparently were *once surrendered* to the will of God and faithfully serving Christ, and then have fallen for women and made shipwreck of their lives through moral delinquency—fornication and adultery.

There was King Uziah In II Chronicles (chapter

26) we read of him, "Sixteen years old was Uzziah when he began to reign, and he reigned fifty and two years in Jerusalem . . . and he did that which was right in the sight of the Lord . . . and he sought God . . . and as long as he sought the Lord, God made him to prosper . . . and his name spread far abroad; for he was marvellously helped, till he was strong. But when he was strong, his heart was lifted up to his destruction: for he transgressed against the Lord his God, and went into the temple of the Lord to burn incense upon the altar of incense. And Azariah, the priest, went in after him . . . and said unto him, 'It appertaineth not unto thee, Uzziah, to burn incense unto the Lord, but to the priests the sons of Aaron, that are consecrated to burn incense: go out of the sanctuary; for thou hast trespassed' . . . Then was Uzziah wroth . . . and while he was wroth with the priests, the leprosy even rose up in his forehead . . . and, behold, he was leprous in his forehead, and they thrust him out from thence . . . because the Lord had smitten him. And Uzziah the king was a leper unto the day of his death, and dwelt in a several (separate) house, being a leper; for he was cut off from the house of the Lord." This good king deterred from the will of God and was very sorely chastened as a result, though he retained his throne till his death.

Consider also Abraham. God had a specific plan and purpose in Abraham, namely to make him the father of the chosen nation. But, being in perplexity because he and Sarah had no children, and wondering how God's purpose was to be carried out, he took the Egyptian maid, Hagar, as his concubine and had a child by her. This erring from the will of God caused untold havoc, first in Abraham's own household between the two women and later between the two children. Later, serious trouble resulted between the Ishmaelites and the Israelites. The trouble in Palestine the past thousand years, and until today, is still between them (the Arabs are Hagar's seed, the descendants of Ishmael). Out of the Arabs came also the terrible scourge of Mohammedanism, which has been a spiritual blight and a curse upon the world, opposing the Gospel of Christ in many lands and slaughtering thousands and thousands of Christians who refused to bow to its commands. Abraham missed God's perfect will at one important point and the world today still reaps the tragic results! Who knows what the price may be if you, too, miss God's will in your life?

Some of these men failed to do God's will through lack of surrender, some through human weakness, some through open disobedience, and some through doubt and bewilderment, as in Abraham's case, but the results were much the same. It is possible for God's people still, for these same causes—lack of surrender, human weakness, deliberate disobedience, or lack of understanding—to miss the perfect will of God. Let us beware lest we be in that sorrowful company. It is possible to miss the way. It is possible to miss His will. It behooves us to "walk circumspectly, not as fools, but as wise . . . understanding what the will of God is" and walking in it.

3

TO MISS HIS PLAN IS TO MISS THE ABUNDANT LIFE

THE KIND OF LIFE God wants His people to enjoy is the *abundant life*. Jesus said, "I am come that they might have *life,* and that they might have it more *abundantly,"* John 10:10. He said many other things along the same line: *"Peace I leave with you,* my peace I give unto you: not as the world giveth, give I unto you. Let not your heart be troubled, neither let it be afraid," John 14:27. "He that abideth in Me, and I in him, the same bringeth forth *much fruit,"* John 15:5. "If ye abide in Me, and My words abide in you, ye shall *ask what ye will, and it shall be done unto you. Herein is my Father glorified, that ye bear much fruit,"* John 15:7, 8. "These things have I spoken unto you, *that my joy might remain* in you, and that *your joy might be full,"* John 15:11. "Whosoever drinketh of the water that I shall give him shall *never thirst;* but . . . shall be in him a *well of water springing up* into everlasting life," John 4:13, 14. "He that believeth on me . . . out of his innermost being shall flow *rivers of living water,"* John 7:38. In Psalm 23 David gives a picture much the same: "I shall not want. He maketh me to lie down in green pastures: He leadeth me beside the still waters. He restoreth my soul . . . I will fear no evil: thy rod and thy staff they comfort me . . . my cup runneth over."

Do not all these and many other Scriptures promise and point to an abundant Life for the people of God? In them one sees abounding life, perfect abiding peace, rich fruitfulness, glory toward God, radiant abiding joy, inward soul-satisfaction, an overflowing experience; as David pictures it, an overflowing cup, for this life and through eternity.

Such a life is the heritage and potential possession of all God's children. He has provided it for them, promised it to them, and is desirous that they should have it. Why then do so few Christians actually experience this abounding life? Why do so many grovel in the dust, never finding full satisfaction in Christ? Why do so few seem to enjoy communion with the Lord? In other words, why don't all believers know this Abundant Life in Christ so often referred to in the Bible and in Christian testimony? The answer is, they are not living in or according to the will of God.

When a Christian walks apart from the perfect will of God, whether through human weakness, deliberate disobedience, or lack of knowledge of that will, he can never know the joy of the Abundant Life. Can a wife who is unfaithful to her marriage vows and disloyal to loving desires of a devoted husband enjoy intimate and unmarried fellowship with him? Can a disobedient son have perfectly happy fellowship with his father whose will he is transgressing? Can a business partner have perfect association and right fellowship with his colleague whose will and desires he constantly ignores and violates? Can friend hold fellowship with friend when there is indifference on the part of one to the will of the other, or the deliberate transgression of personal wishes? Surely the Christian who is not living in obedience to the will of God for his life cannot experience the full blessings and joy of the Christian life. This is almost axiomatic.

The Christian life when lived up to its full privilege and divine desire will embrace at least three things: (1) Gratification of all the inner longings of one's own herat—Self-ward, Psalm 23:5; 63:5,6; 107:9; John 4:13,14; 7:37,38; 14:27, etc.; (2) Glorification of God—God-ward, John 15:8; Matt. 5:16; I Cor. 6:20; Eph. 1:6; (3) Salvation, edification and blessing to other people—Man-ward, Acts 4:13; 9:15; I Cor. 4:9; II Cor. 4:10,11; Gal. 1:16; 6:10; Phil. 1:20; Luke 24:47, 48, etc. The fuller our submission and conformity to the will of God is, the fuller will be the measure of all three of these things in and through our lives. And the less our conformity to that will, the smaller will be their measure. This can be readily understood.

1

The benefits of the glorious Gospel of Christ are intended by Almighty God to fully meet and satisfy all the inner longings of the human heart. "They which do hunger and thirst after righteousness," said Christ, "shall be filled" (Matt. 5:6). The collation of Scriptures we have already given abundantly proves this. The human soul was so created by God that it cannot find rest and satisfaction in anything in this material world or earthly life. Only by reconciliation to God in Christ and by conformity to the divine will of God in Christ Jesus (I Thess. 5:18) can the human soul find peace and satisfaction. There is the *"joy of salvation"* and *"peace with God"* that comes as a result of reconciliation. But there is also "the *joy unspeakable"* and the "peace *from God"* that comes as we walk daily in His presence and do His holy will. A saved person, not walking in obedience to His will may still have peace *with* God, but not have the peace *of* God ruling in his heart, or the joy of Christ filling and flooding his soul. If you want the peace of God to rule in your heart (Col. 3:15), the *will of God* must rule in your life.

Many, many Christians today, who hardly give a thought to the matter of God's will in their lives, know little or nothing about that life of sweet peace and deep inner satisfaction in Christ. They are strangers to the rest that remaineth for the people of God (Heb. 4:9). Nor can such ever know it. Christians read about men like Hudson Taylor and George Mueller and feel that the kind of life those men lived is beyond them. But what, after all, *was* the secret of their lives? Was it not their dominating passion to know and do the will of God, at whatever cost? They were willing to pay the price. Did they reap a worthwhile reward? Were the returns worth the sacrifice? Do we today pity such men? Do we not rather envy them? They found out that there is no Abundant Life for the saint apart from the will of God. And what they found to be true in their lives is *true for all*.

As to glorifying God Himself, it hardly need be said
that no life can accomplish that unless lived in conformity, in a fair degree at least, to His perfect will.
As a disobedient son cannot honor his earthly father,
so a child of God cannot glorify the heavenly Father
while ignoring or transgressing His will. And, after
all, the great object of God in our redemption, was
that men, fallen and disgraced by sin and departure
from the divine purpose, might be "to the praise of the
glory of His grace," (Eph. 1:6, 12). He in the beginning made man in his own image that man might be
the glory and crown of His entire creation. When sin
entered all this was changed. The image of God in man
was sadly defaced, in fact all but erased, and humanity
has become the very shame and scandal of God's creation. Apart from redemption the victory in mankind
would be Satan's. Now through the redemption that
was wrought in Christ and by Christ, depraved and
sinful men may again be restored to fellowship with
God and actual divine-likeness. This was the great
divine purpose in salvation. But, when the twice-born,
twice-created, blood-bought Christian fails to walk in
obedience and conformity to that plan and purpose
which God has marked out for him, God's own heart
is grieved and His holy name suffers shame, or at least
fails to receive the glory due it from that life. This,
Christian friend, is something you will do well to
ponder. Is your life a source of joy and praise to God?
Or is it the occasion of grief and shame to Him? Does
it radiate His grace, or disgrace? Is it a trophy of
regeneration or a travesty upon redemption? Are you

pleasing or grieving the indwelling Holy Spirit? Honoring or dishonoring the precious name of Christ your Saviour? The greatest source of grief and dishonor to God in any Christian's life is indifference and unconcern regarding His will. Love always desires to please. If we really love God we will desire to know His will above all else in order that we "might walk worthy of the Lord unto all pleasing, being fruitful in every good work" (Col. 1:10). "Walk . . . to please God" Paul says in I Thessalonians 4:1.

3

Certainly no one can fail to see that the Christian's life cannot be the fullest measure of blessing and benefit to mankind if not lived in accordance with the will of God. If, for instance, God calls you to South America as a missionary and you fail to comply, you cannot be the means of salvation to the same people you should have been. Or, if you are living a careless, disobedient Christian life, you cannot expect to be the means of salvation-blessing to the lost souls right around you where you now live. With sorrow of heart Paul said to the Jews of his day, "For the name of God is blasphemed among the Gentiles through you" (Romans 2:24). This same horrible fact is true of some Christians today—Christians who have *missed the way*. On the other hand, the same apostle was able to say triumphantly to the Christians of Thessalonica, "Ye were examples to all that believe in Macedonia and Achaia. For from you sounded out the Word of the Lord not only in Macedonia and Achaia, but also in every place your faith to God-ward is spread abroad; so that we need not speak anything" (I Thess. 1:7, 8).

Think of what blessing came to the world through the single life of Paul! Think of the blessing that came to millions of Chinese and to the whole world through the single life of frail little Hudson Taylor! Think of the fruit among men from the life of the shoe cobbler, William Carey! Or, coming closer to our generation, consider the life of D. L. Moody. Mr. Moody, in his early life, heard Henry Varley say that the world had yet to see what God can do through a man who is completely yielded to His will. Then and there Dwight Lyman Moody resolved to be that man. O, that more of us would enter into the resolve to be that man, or that woman! Surely the world *has yet* to see what God can do through a *host* of men and women who are utterly yielded to His will. Is it not a challenge to you, reader, to be one of the number who will go to make up that host? The writer feels keenly this challenge to his own heart as he pens these lines.

To sum up this chapter, to miss God's plan for your life, means to miss the abundant life of personal soul-satisfaction, the life that truly glorifies and pleases God, the life that richly blesses men. In turn, it will result in an unsatisfied Christian experience, a grief to the Holy Spirit and dishonor to the name of Christ, and lack of blessing if not definite occasion of stumbling to our fellow men.

To live according to the will of God is to know *the life that wins.* "It pays to serve Jesus." To miss God's will is to live a life that "Does not pay." Why live such a life?

27

4

GOD DESIRES TO REVEAL HIS WILL TO HIS CHILDREN

THE FACT STATED in the title to this section may seem like a contradiction to actual experience to many Christian people. *Many* have the idea that God is slow and reluctant to let them know His will. They think they have to more or less beg or *force* out of God the revelation of His will for their lives. And, I must confess very frankly, that in my own experience there have been times when that spirit has laid hold of my heart too. Thank God it is no longer so.

But when one stops to reason and meditate on the matter he recognizes at once that God surely would not deliberately withhold from His children the knowledge of His will. Such a thing is unthinkable, really. If the will of God be the all-important factor in our Christian living, and if the knowledge and execution of His will on our part be the one thing that pleases and glorifies Him, and if the absence of it be that which blights our testimony and grieves His heart, it is unthinkable that He should refrain from making His will known, or even be slow to do so.

A servant of Christ has said, "Be assured first that

28

you do not need to implore or plead with God to guide you. He wants to. Over and over in Scripture He expresses not only His willingness but his earnest desire to have you trust Him. It is therefore a wrong attitude to think that we must persuade God to lead us." Of this fact you must be positive. No other attitude or idea makes sense. And God is not a God of confusion.

How then shall one reconcile this inescapable fact, that God *longs* to make His will known, with what seems to be an undeniable fact of common experience, that there is much difficulty connected with ascertaining His will for our lives? What is the answer to this? What is the solution to this apparent problem? Where is the spiritual mechanism "out of gear?" Where does the discrepancy lie? What is the trouble? In reply, we quote from W. W. Orr, who has so aptly stated, "If there is failure to ascertain God's will, or a failure to follow that will, the failure will always be a human failure. It will be your failure."

This point we must get settled. The difficulty encountered in finding God's will and plan for our lives lies not with God, but with us. This may sound a little hard and unsympathetic, especially to those who think they are earnestly and unbiasedly seeking to find God's will, but how can a person who has even an elementary understanding of spiritual truth reach any other conclusion? And, reader, if you will patiently follow this book through to the end you will more than likely see this to be the case, and find help. Don't allow Satan to nurture the insidious and detrimental thought in your mind that you are more anxious to know God's will than He is to reveal it. That cannot be, and is not the truth. If we could only see things as they really are I am sure we would recognize that God is far more desirous of making known His will than we are of receiving and obeying it.

While we reserve fuller discussion of the matter for a later chapter, let it be stated here pointedly that one of the chief ministries of the indwelling Holy Spirit in our lives is to guide us into God's will. Every Christian is indwelt by the Holy Spirit. Every saved person's heart, yea his very physical body, is a temple of the Holy Ghost. "What? know ye not," asks Paul, "that your body is the temple of the Holy Ghost which is in you, which ye have of God, and ye are not your own? . . . Therefore glorify God in your body, and in your spirit, which are God's," I Cor. 6:19, 20. In Romans 8:9 the same apostle says, "Now if any man have not the Spirit of Christ, he is none of His." When Jesus first promised the coming of the Spirit to the disciples He said, "When He, the spirit of truth is come, He will guide you into all truth . . . and He will show you things to come (i.e. the path of service that lay ahead of them subsequent to Pentecost) . . . for He shall receive of mine (i.e. Christ's desires and will) and shall show it unto you" John 16:13, 14. It is plain that one of the chief offices of the Spirit in the believer's life is to make known and make real to him the things that Christ desires him to be and do. He is to be the saint's constant Companion, loving Friend, and unfailing Guide. This office He will never fail to perform as we allow Him the room and opportunity, until we stand at last in God's presence, (John 14:16).

A life must be *conditioned,* and in readiness, *before* the specific will of God for it can be revealed. He will not cast His pearls before swine—this is not meant as an affront but is used for forcefulness. Obviously the Holy Spirit cannot direct the life is that is not yielded to Him. He will not arbitrarily seize the reins of your life contrary to your own will. He awaits the time when you, of your own volition and choice, turn those reins over to Him that He might be the guide henceforth. Happy is the day when that is done! Happy is the life in which it has been done!

Sometimes we may struggle long against giving Him full control. In some cases the period of being made ready is a long one. Then, instead of putting a finger where the failure really lies, in our own heart, we, in our impatience, silently seek to roll the blame for the confusion on Him. Shame! Ralph Davis of the Africa Inland Mission once said in our hearing, "If we were as desirous of doing the will of God as we are of knowing the will of God, we would know it."

People think nothing of going to school twelve to eighteen years of their youth to prepare themselves for this earthly life and a secular profession. In fact, we take for granted that it must be that way. Yet how impatient we become when our Heavenly Father graciously and wisely takes all the time justly required to prepare us in advance for the task He has in view for us to perform. We are so inconsistent! If the apple on the tree could speak it might say, "I wish the gardener would pluck me at once and put me wherever I am am to go. I want to fill my mission in the world so badly. Whether it be to fill a quick place in a hungry boy's stomach, whether to be pared, cut and baked in a pie to adorn a banquet table, or whether to be shipped across the sea to alleviate hunger there, I want to know now and be on the way!" On the other hand, below stands the gardener, gazing at that very apple, and saying, "Why is it so slow in ripening? I would so much like to pick it and put it to use as food, but until it is ripe and ready it would only taste bitter. I wish it would hurry and ripen." Do you understand this little parable? You are the apple, God is the gardener. The delay in knowing the disposition in His will and plan for you is not due to negligence or failure on His part. It is due to an unreadiness on your part.

It is impossible to be in the center of God's will without yielding ourselves up and over to the blessed ministries of the Holy Spirit. With some this comes naturally and easily as the inevitable consequence of repentance and conversion. Doubtless it should be that way. But with *most* of God's children it does not seem to be that way. In most lives it seems that this matter of complete yielding to the Holy Spirit has to take place as a spiritual crisis, as definite sometimes as when the person yielded to Christ as a lost sinner to be saved. But regardless of when or under what circumstances it takes place, *take place it must*. The great heart of God yearns to have His holy will made known and carried out in our lives, and the Spirit of God yearns and groans within our redeemed hearts for the same thing. O, for grace to let Him have full control! When that is the case you may rest assured that God's will shall become a settled matter—doubt, confusion, uncertainty will be swept away.

Imagine if you can, a father who desires his son to be well brought up and fulfill a real mission in life, but who is unwilling or reluctant to instruct him. Or think, if you can, of the manager of a business corporation who has a specific job for each employee under his hand, but who refrains from informing them of their particular tasks. Think of a governor or ruler who wants people to obey his laws and respect his orders but who fails to publish or make known what those laws and orders are. You see how ridiculous it is for us even to think of such inconsistencies. Well then, bear in mind that it is even *more ridiculous* for a child of God to entertain the notion that God is reluctant to reveal His will and plan for our lives to us. Such a spirit is an affront to God's intelligence, love, and purity. Away with such false notions!

Paul prayed for the Colossian Christians that they "might be filled with the knowledge of His will in all wisdom and spiritual understanding" and that they might as a consequence "walk worthy of the Lord unto all pleasing, being fruitful in every good work, and increasing in the knowledge of God," Col. 1:9, 10. Our Great Intercessor is likewise so solicitous for us at the Father's right hand.

5

THE FUNDAMENTAL PRINCIPLE OF
THE CHRISTIAN LIFE

WHAT, FUNDAMENTALLY, is the Christian life, and what after all, is a Christian? To have the right attitude and relationship to the divine will of God we must understand the basic principle of the Christian life, and of our Christian living. The reason so many Christians are living below their privileges and out of harmony with the divine will is that they have never had a real grasp of the relationship they actually must bear to God. And *the Christian life is, basically, a relationship with God*. Being a Christian is in itself primarily a matter of being in the right relationship to God. It is not a matter of improving or changing the old life, but rather of receiving and entering into *a new life*. It is a new state of existence. Many things happen when a person gets saved. He is "born again"; he receives a "new life"; he is made "a new creature"; he "is passed from death unto life"; he becomes "the temple of the Holy Ghost;" he is "redeemed"—"bought with a price"; he becomes a "son of God," a "saint," a "servant of God," an "ambassador of Christ," a "worker together with God." All this is wrought in him by the operation of divine grace and power, not by personal merit or effort, and the result of it all is that the person now belongs to God and the one purpose of his life should be to worship, love, honor and serve Him.

We wish here to pick out a single New Testament phrase that, perhaps above all other singular phrases, sets forth the basic principle of the Christian life and the spirit in which it should be lived. It is an expression occurring and reoccurring throughout the entire Book. It is the title that Paul loved above all others and attached to himself in almost every Epistle. That phrase is, *"Servant of Jesus Christ."* It occurs variously, "Servant of God," "Servant of the Lord," "His Servant," etc. In this expression lies hidden a truth that every believer ought to recognize, and must recognize before he will get far in the matter of executing the will of God.

What does "servant" signify? Not simply an employee, hired to do a particular job for a consideration of a certain wage or reward, as our common thinking today would conclude. Servants in our land are *hired servants,* and the service they render is merely a "bargain" entered into, involving only a certain portion of their time. This is not at all what the New Testament implication of the word "servant" is. We certainly dare not "bargain" with Christ to give him a certain portion of our time, talents, or treasure, in exchange for a certain reward at the end. Perish such a thought, or motive!

The New Testament word is the Greek word "doulos." Far from having any such meaning in it as a hireling, it means simply, and solely, a bond-servant, *a slave.* This is the exact meaning; there is no other. Read some of the New Testament expressions with this literal rendering and note the result: Romans 1:1, "Paul, a bondslave of Jesus Christ"; Romans 6:17, 22, "But God be thanked, though ye were the bondslaves of sin, ye became the bondslaves of righteousness . . . But now being made free from sin, and become bondslaves to God, ye have your fruit unto holiness"; James 1:1, "James, a bondslave of God"; I Corinthians 7:22, "For he that is called in the Lord being a bondslave, is the Lord's freeman: likewise also he that is called, being free, is Christ's bondslave," etc.

1

Two things in particular characterize a slave. A *bondslave is a bought slave,* one who has been bought for a price. He does not belong to himself, or even to his own loved ones. He is not his own. He belongs to his master, solely and entirely. This is exactly the relationship we as Christians bear to Christ. This is precisely what Paul says in I Cor. 6:19, "What? know ye not . . . that ye are *not your own?* For ye *are bought* with a price: therefore glorify God in your body and in your spirit, which are God's." Note a similar statement in 7:23 of the same Epistle, "Ye are bought with a price; be not ye therefore servants (slaves) of men." In I Pet. 1:18 we read, "Ye know that ye were not redeemed with corruptible things, as silver and gold . . . But with the precious blood of Christ, as of a lamb without blemish and without spot." II Pet. 2:1; "There shall be false teachers among you, who privily shall bring in damnable heresies, even denying the Lord who bought them." Hebrew 9:12 says, "By His own blood He . . . obtained eternal redemption for us." The souls of the redeemed in Glory sing, "Thou . . . hast redeemed us to God by Thy blood of every kindred and tongue and people and nation" (Rev. 5:9).

As Christians, therefore, we are not our own, and do not belong to ourselves nor to other people, not even to our own loved ones. This is contrary to the popular attitude and to common Christian thinking today. But it is true nevertheless, surely, solemnly, inescapably true. Our talents are not ours to do with as we please, or as our people please. Our time is not ours to spend as we choose, or as other may wish. All is His. Our spirits are His. Our bodies are His. Our minds, our intelligence, are His. Our talents are His. Our possessions are His. Our children are His. All we are, all we have, all we hold dear, are His and His alone. We *are His blood-bought people;* the Church of Christ is a blood-bought band.

The price He paid for us was "high," far too high. We were a "dear" purchase—in both meanings of the word! Surely it was not a good "bargain" Christ made when He paid His own life and shed His very own blood to redeem me. He got a bad bargain when He finally got possession of me too. But, thank God, it was not a commercial transaction with Him. It was a transaction of love, His own unfathomable love, that love that passes all knowledge. We read in the Word, *"He loved us and gave Himself for us."* It was not what we were worth in ourselves, but what we were worth to His own fathomless love, that led Him to shed His blood for our redemption.

But the fact remains, *He bought us and we belong to Him.* Dare we withhold ourselves from the One who bought us and Whose we actually are? When a Christian "surrenders" or "consecrates" his life to the Lord it is not, after all, any unusual or heroic act, for he belonged to the Lord all the while, body, soul, time and talent. He has merely turned over to God by volitional act that which rightfully belonged to Him all the time! Is this not but the logical and inevitable thing to do? Should this not be the natural act of every child of Christ? Are we doing some outstanding favor or deed to God when we "surrender" to Him that which is but rightfully His by virtue of creation and redemption?

The godly Church of England clergyman, the Reverend Hubert Brooke, in his challenging book, "Personal Consecration," makes this pointed statement, "The Purchaser has, therefore, the right of control over the purchase; and He demands its exercise to be full: 'Ye are not your own—therefore glorify God in your body and in your spirit, which are His.' Personal consecration is the natural result, the obvious fruit, the logical end of the pardon imparted and acceptance granted by God through the death of Jesus Christ. No one who recognizes the cost at which these blessings were obtained, and the principle on which they were given, can have a doubt as to what the issue ought to be in the lives which enjoy these gifts. *It becomes a mere matter of honesty, that that which belongs to the Lord by right of purchase, should be yielded up to Him by the willing choice and deliberate surrender of the purchased possession."*

2

The other thing that stands out about a bondslave is this: *A slave has no will of his own,* only that of his master. He is not free to make his own choices. He is not the director of his own life. He may not choose his own type of work, his master does that. He does not select his place of residence, he goes where his master sends him. He does not arise in the morning at the hour he chooses, he rises when his master says he must. He does not retire at night when he elects to, it is when his master says he may. He is not a free man, he is a bondman. His whole life must be subject to his master's will and wish. His life, his time, his talents are not his own to do with as he chooses; all are at the disposition of his master. Rev. Brooke further says, "Personal consecration bears on ourselves, our lives and homes, our surroundings and possessions; till nothing is left untouched by His all-embracing and all-absorbing claims . . . the subject therefore includes everything which a person claims as or calls his own."

This, Christian, is the relationship you actually bear to Christ. Have you recognized it? Are you living in the light of it? Is this the spirit by which you live? O, if only Christian men and women in our land could grasp this view of the Christian life! There would be no shortage of soul-winners. There would be no lack of missionaries for the foreign fields, or workers at home. There would be no lack of money for God's work. There would not be endless jealousies and quarrelings among the saints. There would be more than a mere handful at prayer meeting to fellowship there with the Lord. Neither would there be all this confusion as to what God's will is for people's lives—if they were surrendered utterly and fully to Christ in the light of this *they would learn His will.*

But you may feel that this is an unattractive picture of the Christian life. Some would say such a life would be a life of bondage. Precisely so. But it is to be *a bondage of love*. I have personally been living in a *social* bondage for the past nineteen years. For, nineteen years ago, in the presence of a minister of the Gospel as well as some other witnesses, and in the presence of Almighty God, I held a young lady's hand and vowed that, richer or poorer, for better or worse, in sickness or health, I would forsake all other persons on earth, even my own father and mother who sacrificed to rear me, and cleave to her only until death should part us. What could be more binding than that? Where could one find worse bondage than that? Do I say "worse" bondage? Ah, no, rather I would say, "Could there be a sweeter bondage?" For, you see, it has been through the years and still is, *a bondage of love*. And if I had it all to do over again I would seek out the same fair young lady, ask her the same question, hope for the same answer, and repeat the same binding vows!

When we realize in daily experience that bondage to our Saviour is love-bondage, the very relationship becomes unutterably precious. His yoke is easy and His burden is light. He is not a cruel taskmaster like Satan, but a loving Master whose will shall only impose upon His servants that which will ultimately be for their own gratification, His glory, and the good of others. Let us first *recognize* this relationship as revealed through the Word; then let us *realize* it in our daily life and experience. God grant it to be so with you, reader.

6

HOW TO KNOW GOD'S WILL

PRELIMINARY CONSIDERATIONS

WE COME NOW to the all-absorbing question: How can one find out God's specific will for his life? What we have said thus far should surely have convinced us that *there is a way to know that perfect will*. In fact, no other conclusion can possibly be reached. But, the great question is—HOW? HOW TO KNOW?

Will God speak to us in some miraculous or supernatural way and tell us what His will for us is? Many are bewildered on this point. They have read in the Scriptures how God appeared in miraculous ways to men and spoke to them in an audible voice, and they conclude that He must deal with them in the same way. God appeared to Abraham in physical form and talked to him regarding His will and plan for his life. He appeared to Moses in a burning bush that was not consumed and in audible language made known His exact will. He sent an angel down from heaven to impart the instruction to Gideon. He called Samuel by name in a human voice in the hours of the night and revealed to him what he was to do. He appeared to Paul in a blinding light which shone above the brightness of the

41

midday sun and He spoke personally to him; again at a later time He called him to Macedonia in a spectacular "vision." To many of the Old Testament leaders and prophets He appeared in visions and revealed His mind to them in that way.

Must we expect something like this? Must we have such an unusual and supernatural revelation before we can rightly know God's will? Will such an experience come to us if we are spiritual and earnest in our desire for the divine will in our lives? Some sincere Christians think so. They feel that one cannot be sure of the will of God without some such parallel experience.

The opening thought of the Epistle to the Hebrews is striking. It says: "God who at sundry (various, olden) times and in divers (diverse, different) manners (methods, ways) spake in times past unto the fathers by the prophets (i.e. in the old dispensation) hath in these last days spoken to us by (Greek "in") His Son." The implication of this Scripture is that though God spoke in those various ways to the ancients, He has in Christ now in this dispensation ceased to do so. God had to resort to the supernatural in giving His Word, the Bible, to the world, and the Bible is of course a supernatural, miraculous revelation, every word directly inspired; but when the scriptural revelation was completed God ceased largely from that type of speaking to men. Christians now have the completed written Revelation from God where His general will is revealed. They also have the indwelling presence of the Holy Spirit in their hearts, who through the Word and through deep mental impressions as we walk with God, guides as to God's specific will.

While God may have to resort to the supernatural

methods at times to reveal His will to some persons, He does not usually do so. It is no sign of deeper spirituality when He does so. Certainly it is no compliment to any Christian if God has to knock him down, or blind him, or bring him into some kind of a trance, or reduce him to some condition of extremity, in order to reveal His will to him. It may be a sign that he was stubborn and rebellious and that only by some drastic means could God therefore speak to him. Certainly this was the case with Paul on the road to Damascus— it was due to his bitter opposition to the Saviour that he had to be met thus. Not all those who were converted in the Book of Acts had that kind of experience; in fact, none of the others did. Peter had to be put into a trance and shown the vision of the sheet in order to be willing to take the message of salvation to the house of Cornelius because of his strong and bitter Jewish prejudice against the Gentiles. That was no compliment to Peter. God employs ordinary means to accomplish His purposes whenever the ordinary means prove sufficient. He employs the extraordinary and miraculous when He sees that it is necessary. Because God has revealed His will to *some* people in that way, it does not follow that He will always, or even generally, do it thus.

The question of modern-day miracles is often raised. While it is not our purpose in this treatise to deal with that, let us simply state that God will work a miracle when He sees it is necessary to work a miracle. If, by way of example, some godly missionary, in an isolated jungle station where no medical aid is available, should contract a deadly disease, God might step into the picture with a miracle and heal that person without medicine. But if the same missionary contracted the disease where medical aid was at hand and available, and he refused to take it, it is likely he would die of the same disease. God resorts to the extraordinary means only when the ordinary one will not suffice.

This principle applies in the matter of God's making His will known to us. He will guide us through the regular means He has established for the purpose, (which we shall come to in our discussion presently), whenever the Christian has sufficient spiritual capacity to make use of them.

One of the great factors involved in determining the divine will is TIME. We frequently sing "Take time to be holy," but are not willing to take the time that it takes in order to be holy. And truly it takes time to be holy! And God can only reveal His will to holy people. Unholy people are in no position to know His will for the simple reason that they are not in readiness to do it. James McConkey has said, "There is no *royal road* to guidance. It is taught only in *God's school*. And there it can be learned. We must be willing to sit on the primary benches, if necessary, to master all its lessons. For guidance is one of the severest tests of the Christian's walk with God. It touches his life at every point. Prayer; knowledge of the Word; personal temperament; tendency to haste . . . impatience with delays; *submission* to the will of God *in all matters in question*—all these and many more, become factors in seeking guidance; and they test to the limit our personal walk with God . . .

"Sometimes you draw from the faucet a glass of water which is muddy and turbid. How do you clear it? You place the glass of muddy water on your table. Moment by moment the sediment deposits at the bottom of the glass. Gradually the water becomes cleared . . . brought about simply by *waiting*. The law is the same in the realm of guidance. Here too, God's great precipitant is—waiting . . . as we do so the sediment in our turbid water slowly settles. . . . The trifling things assume their proper subordinate place. The big things loom up into their proper importance. Waiting is . . . the supremely essential factor. The vast majority of our mistakes come from neglect of it. Haste is more often a trap of Satan than it is a necessity of guidance." We shall have some more important things to say about this in Chapter IX. We conclude this paragraph by quoting some Scriptures: "Let not them that wait upon thee be ashamed (confused)" (Ps. 25:3). "Wait I say upon the Lord" (Ps. 27:14). "Wait on the Lord, and keep his way, (i.e. walk in the light of the Word) and he shall exalt thee to inherit the land (i.e. bring you into the place He has promised and purposed for you)" (Ps. 37:34). "Behold, as the eyes of servants look unto the hand of their master (for direction, as well as provision) and as the eyes of a maiden unto the hand of her mistress; so our eyes wait upon the Lord" (Ps. 123:2).

The one great outstanding passage of Scripture that deals specifically with the matter of how to know the will of God is Romans 12:1, 2: "I beseech you therefore brethren, by the mercies of God, that ye present your bodies a living sacrifice, holy, acceptable unto God, which is your reasonable service. And be not conformed to this world: but be ye transformed by the renewing of your mind, that ye may prove what is that good, and acceptable, and perfect will of God." Note that Paul closes this oft-repeated and heart-searching injunction with the statement, "That ye may *prove what is* that good and acceptable and perfect will of God." "Prove" means to establish the certainty of a thing. It means to determine for sure; to know beyond doubt, to fix, settle. In the Greek the word bears the meaning, "To test and find out, to know by testing." There is in this the thought of knowing God's will by experiment, by experience. It cannot be known merely by an intellectual process, but through deep spiritual experience. If we would certainly, assuredly, doubtlessly, know God's will for our lives we must analyze carefully what the Apostles say in this great injunction, and then follow the instructions given. If we are not sufficiently sincere to obey these instructions we are not sufficiently in earnest about desiring God's will. So now let us proceed to analyze Romans 12:1, 2.

7

HOW TO KNOW GOD'S WILL (Cont.)

PREPARATORY STEPS: SURRENDER

A CAREFUL STUDY of Romans 12:1-2 shows that the Apostle Paul marks out therein three preparatory steps that *must be taken* in order "that ye may *prove what is* . . . that good and acceptable and perfect will of God."

The first of these steps is clearly carved out in the words, "Present your bodies a living sacrifice." This means utter, unreserved, unqualified surrender. According to Paul, such utter surrender to God as a living offering on His altar of sacrifice is the first prerequisite toward the knowing of His will. He plainly and pointedly says, "Present your bodies a living sacrifice . . . that ye may prove what is that . . . perfect will of God." This is inspired instruction, this is holy writ, this is God's Word—this, therefore, cannot be ignored or sidestepped. To do so means to close the door to a knowledge of His will and to *miss the way*. This writer a few years ago, desiring to have something clear and direct from the Word of God itself on the matter of how to know the divine will to pass on to a group of Christian young people whom he had been asked to address on the subject, earnestly sought the help of the Spirit for scriptural light. He believes the Spirit Himself pointed him to this great passage. Since that time the passage has been a challenge for successful personal guidance on numerous occasions, and has been used of God in helping others who were seeking. It searches one's heart and challenges one's spiritual status every time it is seriously used. But *it works!* How could it fail? It is God's own instruction on how to know His will.

Let us now examine well this first preparatory step, and ponder it with care.

What does this personal surrender, this presenting of one's self to God as a living sacrifice, involve? To offer a thing in sacrifice means to *give it up* completely, finally, forever. When a sacrifice was made in ancient Israel on the brazen altar, the figure which Paul here employs, were it a sheep, goat, or a calf, it was given up and over to God completely, to be burned with fire, consumed by the priest, or both (i.e. part to each) as the divine statute called for. The offerer could lay no further claim to it, nor to any part of it. It was God's to do with and to make disposition of as His own will and law required. And the disposition of God with reference to the sacrifice could not be effected *until* the worshipper had surrendered it. So must be the surrender of our lives, *our very selves,* to God, if we desire His will to be manifested and wrought out in our lives. All that we are, all that we have, all our desires, plans, affections, choices, sentiments, likes and dislikes, must first be fully and finally surrendered to God in utter submission *before* we can know what His will is, and what He desires and requires of our lives.

48

It is simple and easy to say it. But it is not so simple or easy to do it, *to make the surrender*. And, it is one thing to say you surrender, but quite a different thing to genuinely do it in actual experience. Raising the hand in a meeting, or going to an altar when the call to consecration and surrender is given, does not necessarily mean it has been done. Such manifestations do usually signify, at least, that there is a *need* and *desire* in the heart to surrender, but do not necessarily effect such surrender. Self is very subtle, the human heart is exceedingly deceitful, Satan is amazingly wily. This utter surrender of one's whole life, body and soul, time and talents, is a personal transaction between the soul and God, culminating in an utter yielding of one's own selfish will to God as a result of the Holy Spirit's inward probing and working. It is between you and God alone; no one else can be in on this; the closet door must be shut, the shades drawn; you surrender your will to God's will, your soul and life to God's desire and disposition. There is no way to side-step or by-pass the altar of sacrifice if you would walk in God's court and minister in His sanctuary in accordance to His will.

In her striking book entitled "A, B, C's for Christian Living," Frieda Schneider, invalided and bedridden for the greater part of her life, says, on this matter of surrender: "It is better to yield now than to wait until God puts you on a 'stretcher' as the chiropractor does with his unruly patients. This stretcher method often constitutes an avalanche of crucial circumstances which crush earthly hopes. Therefore, this admonition—prostrate yourself before Christ and invite His nail-scarred hands to adjust your life, correct your spirit . . . Rest YOUR case in His hands. He died for you; now live for Him.

Then you, too, will walk peacefully and profitably with God. Yea, then you will have that blissful sense of His divine current flowing freely through your life. So 'yield yourselves unto the Lord, and enter into His sanctuary, which He had sanctified forever: and serve the Lord your God, that the fierceness of His wrath may turn away from you' (II Chron. 30:8)."

Mr. Orr says, "If I had never yet seen this truth and had not yielded my life to God, this is what I would do. After meditation upon God's invitations in the Bible (Col. 3:1-4), and after careful examination of the sincerity of my own heart, I would tell my Heavenly Father that I wanted Him to fully and completely direct my life from now on. I would further tell him that in view of His love and His omniscience, I was willing to go where He wanted me to go, and be whatever He wanted me to be. I would make this a definite step in my Christian career (Hebrews 12:1, 2), and I would note down this decision in some safe place, perhaps on the fly leaf of my Bible. But that's not all. The very next morning after this complete surrender I would again pour into the ears of my Heavenly Father the same confession, reminding Him that I still meant with all my heart what I had previously said. The next day I would repeat the same and the next day and the next. Why? Will God forget? No, God will never forget, but you may. And this daily commitment is a splendid way to remain *yielded* to God's will." This is good practical spiritual counsel.

Some may regard the complete surrender of all one is and all he holds dear and precious, all his fond plans and private ambitions, upon the altar of sacrifice as too costly a thing. To do such a thing they regard as wholly unattractive or as utterly unreasonable. This is what the inspired apostle himself anticipated. Therefore, he adds, after his appeal, "Which is your *reasonable service."* In view of the great mercies of God to us in Christ, giving His Son as a sacrifice and propitiation for our salvation, so runs the argument of Paul, it is only reasonable that we should give ourselves back to Him for His good will and pleasure. Ponder the words of Frances Ridley Havergal's hymn:

> I gave My life for thee
> My precious blood I shed
> That thou might'st ransomed be,
> And quickened from the dead:
> I gave, I gave My life for thee,
> What hast thou given for Me?
>
> I suffered much for thee,
> More than thy tongue can tell,
> Of bitt'rest agony,
> To rescue thee from hell;
> I've borne, I've borne it all for thee,
> What hast thou borne for Me?
>
> My Father's house of light,
> My glory-circled throne
> I left for earthly night,
> For wand'rings sad and lone;
> I left, I left it all for thee,
> Hast thou left aught for Me?

Another famous hymn writer put it:

> Were the whole realm of nature mine,
> That were a present *far too small:*
> Love, so amazing, so divine,
> Demands *my soul, my life, my all!*

The very word which Paul employs at the outset of his appeal indicates that both he and the Spirit knew how hard it would be for many to take this all-essential step. He says, "I *beseech you,* therefore, brethren, by the mercies of God." What powerful words and language are here! To beseech means to beg, to plead, to implore, to urge with all persuasion possible. He knew it would take this. If God's people could *see* this indispensible step, and really *take* it, most of their problems regarding the knowledge of His will would vanish away. Of this we are personally persuaded. How could it be otherwise if this Scripture holds true as it must? *The matter of knowing God's will is far more a matter of the heart than it is a matter of the intellect,* a heart problem more than a head problem. If our hearts were right, rightly surrendered and rightly related to God, our minds would discern far more readily the guidance of God. May the Spirit Himself, the Blessed Paraclete, cause our souls to hear and heed the divine injunction and instruction in Romans 12:1 and 2! O, that Christians would but take the first great essential, preparatory step, that of *utter surrender.*

Let us quote again from the suffering, saintly Frieda Schneider, "There is absolutely no reason for not yielding ourselves one hundred per cent to the cause of Christ. Wholehearted surrender does many things for us. It is the first clue to a complete resultful life; it puts new vigor into our veins; it makes us loyal under difficulty and discipline; it changes us from a sourpuss to sweetness. In short, complete compliance to Christ's will produces joy here and now as well as in the sweet by and by."

According to this plain passage, *surrender* to God's

will, before one knows what it is or what it may demand, must precede a knowledge of that will. This is God's fixed and revealed order. It cannot be reversed; it cannot be ignored. It is His way. And if we want to know what His will is we must follow His way of revealing it.

As a boy, often when I wanted my brother to do something for me which I feared he would not be pleased or desirous to do, I would try to extract from him the promise to do it before telling him what it was, and then hold him to his promise. I would very simply ask, "Will you promise to do me a favor?" But only too often his quick come-back was, "What is it?" In other words, he was not sufficiently surrendered to me, or devoted to me, or had sufficient confidence in me, to agree to do my will and pleasure *until he knew* what it was. Actually he was not surrendering his will to mine at all! He was only manifesting a kind of interest and readiness to do my pleasure if it did not too severely cross or interfere with his own. That is not real surrender at all. So it is with many Christians. God is, in effect, saying to all His children, "Will you do my will?" and so many of them are coming back with, "What is it, Lord? Tell me what it is so I can decide." And in that response they are really intimating that if the thing God is requesting is something not too much in discord with their own will, something not too contrary to their own liking, they will yield to the doing of it.

Is that the kind of surrender Romans 12:1 implies? Is that surrender at all? In essence, such Christians will not promise to do God's will until He has *first* revealed or submitted a kind of "blueprint sketch" of it to them for their own scrutiny and acquiescence. *This is the reverse of God's divine order* and will not get one far either in the knowing *or* the doing of His holy will. He requires first that we be utterly surrendered and wholly abandoned and given up to do His will, *regardless* of what it proves to be or may demand, before He makes His plan known. Such a submission, such a readiness, is the first preparatory step toward the knowing. Without our taking that first step God is not likely to reveal His will to one. As we said before, not as an affront, but as a spiritual principle, God will not cast the pearls of His will before the swine of selfish, carnal, material, wordly, unsurrendered lives.

As we quote, again from McConkey, note this: *"Will* to do *God's* will for your life instead of your own. Do not launch out upon the sea of life headed for a port of your own choosing, guided by a chart of your own draughting, driven by the power of your own selfish pleasures or ambitions. Come to God. *Yield your life to Him by one act of trustful, irrevocable surrender* . . . So shall you come steadily to know and see God's will for your life . . . Without a shadow of a doubt, we will begin to know God's will as soon as we begin to *choose* His will for our lives instead of our own."

> All to Jesus I surrender, All to Him I freely give.
> I will ever love and trust Him,
> In His presence daily live.
> I surrender all! I surrender all!
> All to Thee my blessed Saviour
> I surrender all.

You have often sung this—but have you ever *done* this?

8

HOW TO KNOW GOD'S WILL (Cont.)

PREPARATORY STEPS: SEPARATION FROM THE WORLD

THERE IS A SECOND IMPORTANT, yes, indispensable step which must be taken before God's will may be known. This also is clearly carved out in the passage we are considering, Romans 12:1, 2. That second injunction, following the one for full surrender, is, "And be not conformed to this world." And, of course, the issue of this as of the entire exhortation in the passage still is, "That ye may prove what is that good and acceptable and perfect will of God." Surely Step Number Two is clearly marked: SEPARATION FROM THE WORLD AND FROM WORLDLINESS.

Here is something of essential importance which thousands of well-meaning young people and other Christians overlook these days: worldliness, worldly conformity, worldly ambitions, worldly living, worldly goals, worldly standards, worldly habits, worldly dress, and worldly pleasures.

It must be stated in all truth and frankness that God does not reveal His specific will to worldly Christians. They are not in a position worthy of His will. They are not ready for it. Quite often my own heart overflows with perplexity and grief as people come to me with the world stamped all over them, literally painted all over their faces, and ask me to pray that God will manifest His will to them regarding specific things in their lives—perhaps their life calling. I am painfully aware that they are not in line to receive the knowledge of His will. The way is blocked by their own love of and conformity to this godless world. It is really vain for a person whose affections are wrapped up in worldly things, and whose life is patterned after worldly standards, and guided by worldly principles, to ask prayer about knowing the will of God. Such prayer is only offered in vain. (For such I always pray rather that God will open their eyes to see their disobedience to God's Word and give them grace to give up and separate from worldly things). God simply cannot reveal His will to such lives.

The pattern God follows in illuminating His people is set forth in this tremendous passage of Scripture we are considering, so well known, and yet withal, so *little* known. That principle is, "Be not conformed to this world . . . that ye may prove what is . . . the will of God." Why does God set forth and abide by such a principle? Why must a Christian be denied the privilege of knowing the divine plan for his life just because he has a love and weakness for some of the things and ways of the world? The answer is quite clear. They are not *prepared* to know God's specific will by virtue of the fact that they are not disposed to do His general will as revealed in the Bible for all Christians. Again we must say, with both love and grief, He will not cast His pearls before swine. The Bible speaks emphatically and repeatedly against God's people loving and following the world: "Love not the world, *neither the things that are in the world. If any man love the world, the love of the Father is not in him*," I John 2:15. "Know ye not that the friendship of the world is enmity with God? Whosoever, therefore, will be a friend of the world is the enemy of God," James 4:4. "We know that we are of God, and *the whole world lieth in wickedness*" (lit., "the wicked one"), I John 5:19. "Jesus Christ . . . gave Himself . . . that He might deliver us from *this present evil world,* according to the will of God and our Father," Gal. 1:4. "Marvel not, my brethren if the *world hate you,*" I John 3:13. "If the world hate you, ye know that it hated me before it hated you. If ye were of the world, the world would love his own: but because *ye are not of the world*, but *I have chosen you out of the world, therefore the world hateth you,*" John 15:18, 19. "I pray not that thou shouldest take them out of the world, but that thou shouldest *keep them from the evil. They are not of the world, even as I am not of the world,*" John 17:15, 16. In the face of these and many more statements of Scripture it is clear that God's people are not to love the world, not to follow the world, not to be conformed to the world, not to be bound up with the world. If Christians ignore these plain exhortations and injunctions of Scripture they certainly are not in a position to have more light revealed to them; they are not walking in the light they already have. No one can reasonably expect more light on this path unless he follows the light that has already been unmistakably given.

So, dear heart, do not deceive yourself, God will not reveal His will and plan to you so long *as you cling to the world*. We must have our hearts and minds fixed in all seriousness upon the things which are above (Col. 3:1-3) and be weaned away from the world before we are really in a position to receive the will of God. This is *an essential step; it cannot be side-stepped.*

What is actually meant by, "Be not conformed to the world?" In other words, what is worldly conformity in the light of Scripture? At least three things are certainly meant.

First: We are not to conform to the world's pattern, or principles. The worldly pattern of life is one of self-ishness, sinfulness and sensuality. The world's principle of life is materialism, greed, and lust. When a young man, for example, goes to South America under some commercial firm with a sizeable salary, the world approves and applauds. "He's a go-getter," they say. "He's got what it takes." "He's going places." "He's really making himself amount to something." But if a young fellow goes to the same country as a missionary for Christ and souls, with eternal values in view, the worldly folks shake their heads in disapproval and bewilderment. "Throwing his life away," they say. "Can't understand why he should be so foolhardy." "What a tragedy!"

Right there one can see the difference between the principle and pattern of a worldling and the true Christian. Only it is sad that too many Christians conform to the same principle. "Blessed is the man," says the first Psalm, "that walketh not after the counsel of the ungodly." That means he doesn't pattern his life and walk after the world's counsel or standards. He, who is conformed to the world, and is interested in living only for himself and for the material things has his eyes blinded to spiritual realities and objectives, and therefore cannot perceive the will of God which is primarily, if not purely, spiritual in its objectives. The will of God has eternal values in view; the worldly pattern embraces only material values. Hence one opposes and eclipses the other. No one who is thus conformed to the world's principle of living, as multitudes of Christians are, can be prepared for a missionary call, for example. His whole life is in contradiction to the idea. So it is a logical fact that one whose life is conformed to the world and whose affections and ambitions are on the things of the world is not in a position to know God's celestial will. One old divine aptly said, "We must *sit loose* to the things of the world." Too many desire to *sit tight* instead. It is sad to see so much of this worldly principle dominating even the Christian ministry in America today; no wonder there is barrenness in our churches.

As to the sins and sensual practices of the world today, surely it is superfluous to say that the Christian must separate himself from the whole setup. Remember I John 5:19, the truth of which is obvious on every hand in our time.

Second: We are not to seek or indulge in the world's pleasures. Hollywood had largely set the pace for the world's pleasures. And what pleasures they are! Hardly a popular pleasure in the land today is untainted by sin, sex or smut of some kind. The world's greatest playhouse perhaps is the theater. It is a known fact that the theater specializes in crime, horror, and sex. It magnifies illicit love affairs, nudism, lustful suggestions, vice of all kinds. The theater is no place for wholesome pleasure, *no place for a saint of God.* Another popular play house is the dance hall. The modern dance is based essentially on one thing: sex, lust. This cannot well be contradicted. How a Christian can participate in dances, how churches can sponsor them, how Christian parents can condone them, is beyond our comprehension! But let not such think they can know or carry out the will of God for their lives. They are already trampling His will under foot! How can they expect any further revelation?

Third: We are not to set our affections on the world's possessions. Sometimes older or better taught Christians severely criticize younger and less enlightened ones for clinging to worldly pleasures, while they themselves are just as guilty of worldliness in the eyes of God by clinging to worldly possessions. One loves its pleasures, the other its treasures, and both are sinful and worldly in the light of God's Word. Many a Christian has missed God's way because he has loved the material things of the world. Many have not been able to see the vision of the mission fields because they are blinded by the "things" of the world. (Usually I John 2:15 is limited in its interpretation to the *pleasures* of the world—remember however there were no movies, no modern dances, etc. in John's time—whereas the verse says the "things" of the world, which includes material possessions, goods, money, etc. People who use this verse need to beware lest it become their boomerang). The rich young ruler missed the way of life because "he had great possessions" (Mark 10:17-22). A fourth part of the seed in the Parable of the Sower represents the one that "heareth the Word; and the care of this world, and the *deceitfulness of riches,* choke the Word, and he becometh unfruitful" (Matt. 13:22). "Ye cannot serve God and mammon (wealth)." How many a Christian young person, and older one too, has missed the path of God's will because he is tied up to worldly possessions and bound by a lust for wealth. Such a person is not in line for further manifestation of the will of God; he is already digressing, yes, transgressing that will.

How much worldly conformity there is today, in all three of these directions! And it is such an effective stumbling block in the way of God's will because people are not aware of its presence. The stone the traveler does not see is the one he is surest to stumble over. So it is with the matter of worldliness and worldly conformity. Multitudes of Christian people are worldly in one of these three aspects, many in all of them, and yet are perfectly oblivious to any fault or failure in their lives, and wonder why God's guidance is not clearer. Perhaps they are not in complete innocence or oblivion, either, for they certainly resent being made aware of the stumbling block, or having some man of God point it out. Some, in fact, become highly indignant if the preacher broaches this exceedingly important subject. Others are merely amused at such sermons, with no thought of taking the matter seriously. Others again appear astonished when told Christians should not patronize theatres, dance halls, card parties, Sunday amusements, or use paint and make-up. The latter was once used exclusively by pagans and was adopted first in civilized lands by harlots and people of the world. Then still others are just plainly indifferent to all such exhortations, like the proverbial pouring of water on a duck's back. And yet Paul makes it clear that we cannot be "conformed to the world" if we desire to determine the true will of God for our lives.

The old puritans and saints of earlier times are ridiculed and frowned upon by religious professors today. Yet all must admit that they found something in salvation and in Christ that most believers seem to be missing today, judging by a comparison between their writings and what one sees in the lives of Christians generally now. *And they produced something for God.* The church they produced was virile and active. It had power in the local communities and respect in the world at large. Men were *converted* in those days, too. The "revivals" produced in the early days of our nation were revivals indeed. There was no expensive advertising, no *"Hollywood evangelism"* with all the worldly glamour and false appeal, no "psychology" methods or long drawn-out appeals for altar call. But *souls were swept into the kingdom of God.* How was it done? What was their secret? What did they do? One thing is certain, *they lived lives of separation from the world.* Whatever else was true of them, this was certainly true. They paid the price of separation, walked in the light and knowledge of God's will, and they had power with men and with God. Maybe if we want that same power we'll have to pay the same price.

What about it? Are you ready? Do you value God's will enough, do you value the knowing of it enough, to "be not conformed to the world?" This is the second preparatory step toward knowing the divine will and we see no way to side-step it or get around it. You can't reach Paul's promise. "That ye may prove," until you get past his proposition, "Be not conformed." Don't try it; to do so will spell failure and confusion. Christian friend, ponder this well.

9

HOW TO KNOW GOD'S WILL (Cont.)

PREPARATORY STEPS: SPIRITUAL-MINDEDNESS

THE THIRD BASIC STEP toward knowing the will of God, as marked out by Paul in Romans 12:1 and 2 is, *"Be ye transformed by the renewing of your mind."* What does this mean? Just what is the step here pointed out? What is the renewing of the mind that has a transforming power and effect upon the believer's life and results in the knowledge of His will? What is really meant by the *"renewing of your mind?"*

An illustration from the experience of a student in school may help us. He goes through a semester of study in a casual and easy-going way; then comes the end of the semester with its inevitable "exams." What does the student do in order to know those things the examination questions may likely call for? How does he prepare? Everyone knows the answer. He sits up far into the night, or even into the wee hours of the morning, poring over his books and notes and racking his brain ruminating over the professor's lectures. He is refreshing, or renewing, his mind by reading and meditating. He tries to live over again those class

63

periods, to renew in his consciousness the things there imparted.

This is precisely what Paul is saying. Our minds, our hearts, our spirits, our entire spiritual lives, must constantly be refreshed by dwelling in Christ's presence and feeding on His Word. Unless there be such a spiritual frame of mind and life God's will cannot be found, for it is by our close communion and fellowship with Him that the Holy Spirit communicates the will of God to our hearts. The will of God can never be known to carnally-minded Christians; He will only make it known to those who are spiritually-minded and whose lives are transformed by constant occupation with the things of the Spirit. In order to have spiritual understanding there must be in us a spiritual frame of mind. *The whole tenor of the life must be spiritual.* There must be a daily, constant walk with God through prayer and the searching of the Word. It is in this way alone that our lives will be renewed, refreshed, transformed, and we shall be "conditioned" *to receive* the knowledge of His will.

In other words, the step the Apostle points out here in the knowing of the Will of God is *Spiritual-Mindedness.* Here then are three steps: *Surrender, Separation from the World, Spiritual-Mindedness.*

Those who do not sufficiently value God's holy will to wait prayerfully on Him for its revelation are unworthy to know it. Before any of us can know that will, we must properly *value* it. The late Rev. Lee H. Downing, missionary to Africa, in his pamphlet, *God's Plan for My Life,* says, "Think over your daily schedule and decide when in the twenty-four hours you could be *alone with the Lord without interruption,* and make up your mind to meet Him every day at that time. The duration of the interview (what a rich term **Downing** here uses) will be determined somewhat by the other duties demanding your attention. A half-hour *daily,* if more cannot be spared, is better than an hour today, no time tomorrow, and such time the day following as can be conveniently spent in this way. *The faithful keeping of this appointment* prepares one to receive impressions from the Lord, and brings the consciousness of having definite dealings with Him . . . In the secret place, shut in with God (Matt. 6:6) we may expect leadings so definite as to assure others we have learned to discern His presence, and to understand His impressions."

It has been the writer's experience and conviction for a number of years, that only as we walk in close and constant fellowship with the Lord, definitely and directly communing with Him through prayer and the Word, can He communicate the knowledge of His will to us. Thus we are forced to the conclusion which has already been propounded that knowing God's will is not so much a problem of the intellect as it is a problem of the heart and life. As we overcome those things that keep us from that vital fellowship with our Saviour, the knowing of His will comes more or less naturally and automatically.

Suppose an employee of a corporation wants instruction from his boss while away from the home office on a company errand. What does he do? What *must* he do? He must establish a line of communication between himself and his chief—by telephone for example. He goes to the telephone, places the call, and establishes the contact which enables him to receive the clear

65

instruction he desires. But if he fails to keep the receiver to his ear, or if he permits his mind to be detracted by some local attraction, or if he falls asleep, or fails to listen, he cannot know his master's will in the given matter. So it is with us as Christians. We must keep in close communication with our Lord, so He can naturally and easily impart to us the knowledge of His will. Such a channel of communication must be maintained by a life of prayer and fellowship with Him.

Mr. Orr, on this point, makes the significant comment: "Prayer becomes a two-way line of communication between a Christian who desires to know the will of God, and a God who desires that His children shall know and fulfill His will. This is one *indispensable factor* in ascertaining the plan and purpose of God for our lives. We should learn to pray without ceasing. Day after day, hour after hour, moment after moment, *the Christian should have his prayer line open.* . . . Prayer is something that should be engaged in constantly all day long. God is not too busy with what He is doing to talk with you continually. The Christian who desires to know the will of God should learn the fine art of uninterrupted prayer."

My own experience of twenty-four years as a Christian has revealed to me that there is no streamlined recipe, or short-cut way, to finding our God's will. After this quarter of a century of knowing the Lord, my experience is even as it was at the beginning of my spiritual life: when I allow my fellowship with the Lord to grow cold I am in hopeless difficulty in determining His will and in making important decisions; when I walk in conscious, abiding fellowship with Him,

I seem to know just what He would have me do in any given thing. *But it takes time.* Don't forget that. Walking with God is not an experience of a few hours, nor days, but of months and years. Over and over in Scripture we are exhorted to "wait" on God for His blessings and guidance: If His guidance is worth anything it is worth waiting for. To wait on God implies, of course, a waiting in prayer, fellowship, and communion, not a cold marking of time. It is by this continual and prayerful waiting upon Him that our hearts are *conditioned* for His will, so that when it is revealed it may likewise be carried out.

All this is quite in contrast to the strange experience, if we may call it that, of many Christians today. They allow themselves to be so entangled by duties and things that they have little time or disposition to sit at Jesus' feet and learn of Him. Then when an emergency arises in their lives they want to rush into the Lord's presence, throw themselves at His feet, and pray something like this (if their prayer were really analyzed): "Lord Jesus, I've been awfully busy and haven't had much time to talk or visit with you. Forgive me. But now, Lord, I'm in a predicament, and I must know your will in this very important matter by 10 o'clock tomorrow morning. So please, Lord, hurry up, and reveal it to me. Amen." This will never do! His will is not revealed in that way, nor, indeed, to such lives. But if we live daily in His presence, and walk continually in His fellowship, when the emergency arises, we will have the experience of the prophet who said, "Thine ear shall hear a voice behind thee, saying, this is the way, walk ye in it, when ye turn to the right hand, and when ye turn to the left" (Isaiah 30:21).

When a husband and wife live in the right relationship together over a period of years there develops between them on the part of each the knowledge of the other's will and desires. The wife need not go into long and laborious details in revealing her will to her lover; a mere word, or even a certain look, or gesture, suffices. They have come to know and understand each other. So it is also between a mother and her child. The little one is quick to grasp her will and desire because he has lived daily with her and has run errands for her before. *When two persons love one another and live with one another intimately, the one has little difficulty discerning the other's pleasure and will.* How precisely true this is in our spiritual experience with the Lord! But on the other hand, when a separation occurs between a husband and wife, either literally, or in heart and spirit, that mutual understanding grows dim. If such a condition be allowed to continue over a period of months or years it may disappear altogether and the understanding of one's will by the other will be like finding out the will of one who is a total stranger. If Christ be merely the Saviour of your soul, but so far as your daily life is concerned, only a "stranger," naturally you will encounter greater difficulty acquiring a knowledge of His will for your life.

Steward's book, *God in Our Street,* though definitely liberal in its theology, contains one statement in the last chapter which is *challenging:* "Drummond pointed out to the students of Edinburgh what he called the 'lesser mileposts to the understanding of the will of God.' These include opportunity, circumstances, happiness, the wishes of parents, the advice of friends, the evaluation of one's own abilities, personal inclination, the needs of the day, and conscience. . . . But these are not always sure guides. It is through prayer, deep and searching, in which the Spirit of God helps us sort our loyalties and arrange our values, that we find the greatest discovery of all—the will of God for character and career—and have released within us not only the intelligence, and the will, but the deep . . . emotions which can carry us through to the doing of the task." Later on, he says, on the New Testament Apostles, "Jesus said, 'It is expedient for you that I go away.' There comes a day when the young eagle must be pushed from the nest, when the child must face life alone, when the apprentice becomes a journeyman, leaves the master's shop to carve out his own career in the big world. That time came at Pentecost." It was at Pentecost that the Holy Spirit was "given" to the church *to empower and direct* the believers in their lives and labors for Christ.

The well-known New Testament benediction embraces "the communion of the Holy Ghost," II Cor. 13:14. What does this mean? It is something important enough in spiritual experience to be ranked along with "the grace of the Lord Jesus Christ, and the love of God." In this glorious benediction one actually comes face to face with the three cardinal facts of the Gospel: the Love of God, the source of our salvation; the Grace of Jesus Christ, the channel; and the Communion of the Holy Spirit, the issue of it all, i.e. the believer's resultant life and experience. Brethren, ponder this. It is through the communion of the indwelling Holy Spirit that God's children have the knowledge of His will communicated to them. We shall say more about this in Chapter XI.

Comparatively few people on this side of the Atlantic seem to know much about the life and ministry of the godly soul, Blumhardt, across the water. He has long since gone to be with the Lord. He seemed to have been given a special ministry of praying for the sick and his prayers were signally honored by God. Before praying for a sick person, however, it was his custom to wait upon the Lord alone to ascertain His will regarding the healing of that particular individual. It was his testimony that when he first began doing this it frequently took him hours to determine the Divine Will in a given case. But after a couple of years had passed this way, he stated that he could turn to God in prayer regarding a sick or afflicted person and the answer would come almost immediately. Blumhardt had learned by much experience in prayer how to know the mind of God in the matter of healing. This should be a real lesson to us that divine guidance is learned only by a close, continuous, experimental walk with Him. And such a walk is, after all, the very source of the Christian's own daily joy and fulness of blessing. Any other kind of a Christian walk is fraught with peril. For, let not God's child forget that there are evil spirits in the world whose business and occupation it is to deceive and lead them astray. Only by this experimental knowledge that comes as we walk prayerfully with our Saviour can we be preserved from the danger of the insidious misleading of those false, deceiving spirits. Study in this connection I John 4:1.

James McConkey in his pamphlet *The God-Planned Life,* tells about the founder of the Clifton Springs Sanitarium, Dr. Henry Foster, who was a man of mighty power with God. He was, too, a man of marvelous insight into the mind and ways of God as pertains to guidance in the affairs of life. Visitors who came to the sanitarium, after his decease, were wont to ask an old physician on the staff what the secret of Foster's life was. He would then take the visitor upstairs to Dr. Foster's former office and, pointing to two ragged holes in the carpet, worn there by the knees of that dear saint, would say, "That, sir, was the secret of Henry Foster's power and wisdom in the things of God and men." McConkey then comments, "Friend, when your bedroom carpet begins to wear out after that fashion, the man who lives in that room need not have any fear about missing God's life-plan. *For that is the open secret* of wisdom and guidance in the life of every man. . . . 'Does any man lack wisdom? Let him ask of God.' Are you one of the men who lack wisdom concerning God's plan for their lives? Then ask of God. Pray! Pray trustfully, pray steadily, pray expectantly, and God will certainly guide you into that blessed place where you will be as sure you are in His chosen pathway as you are of your salvation." Surely the thing Mc-Conkey is here talking about is precisely what Paul was referring to when he said, *"Be ye transformed by the renewing of your mind."* An inevitable by-product of such a continual walk with God and constant refreshing and revival of soul, is the transforming of the whole life. Of Christ it was said, on the Mount of Transfiguration, "As He prayed the fashion of His countenance was altered." This has always been true of His people; it must, and will, be true of us today.

Dr. Harold R. Cook, head of the Department of Missions of the Moody Bible Institute of Chicago, has listed in a very fine article he published in *Moody*

Monthly, August, 1949, as the general principles of divine guidance: "A recognition of the need for guidance, a willingness to be led, a deliberate renunciation of a self-interest, a *close walk with God so as to be sensitive to His wishes,* as well as a constant use of the Word of God in earnest prayer." While the emphasized line is not so done in Dr. Cook's own article, it is doubtless the heart and crux of the whole matter in actual experience. Those who are willing to pay the price of a true walk with God will gain the precious treasure of the sure knowledge of His perfect will for their lives. And, as James McConkey stated, this is the open secret!

Reader, this is perhaps the most important chapter of our little book. Ponder it well, pour over its contents, above all, practice its truths. *Practice the presence of Christ.*

10

SOURCES OF GUIDANCE

THE WORD OF GOD

THE KNOWLEDGE of God's will indeed represents life on the highest spiritual plane. Lack of the knowledge and assurance of that will means to live on a lower spiritual plane. Certainly these two facts are obvious. But the perennial question is, How can one get from the lower plane of uncertainty to that higher plane of assurance? In order to get from the ground-level floor of our homes to the second story we install stairways, a series of steps, each one of which elevates one toward the higher floor. Now, if I should be visiting in a home, and should inquire of my host where the washroom was, and he would reply that it was on the second floor, the understanding would be that I must use the stairs to get up there. If I should refuse to do that and start looking around the house for some other way or means of getting up there, I am sure my host would think me a very peculiar man. If I should tell him I objected to going up steps, because it was hard work, he would doubtless tell me it was the easiest way they had of getting to the second floor of their home!

73

Now the only way to get from the lower plane of doubt and uncertainty concerning the will of God in your life, to that higher plane of assurance, is to traverse the three steps we have pointed out in the three preceding chapters. If some object to taking these steps because they are hard, we reply that there is no other way to arrive at the knowledge of God's will. God has not provided spiritual *"elevators"* to automatically lift people up to that higher plane of spiritual knowledge! Many would indeed like to get there by the elevator method, instantaneously and without any effort on their part, but we are persuaded no such method exists. You cannot arrive at the knowledge of His will without taking those three upward steps of Romans 12:1, 2 any more than you can arrive at the second floor of an ordinary home without employing the stairs provided for the purpose. To refuse to go up the steps means to stay on the same lower plane.

But, if one has truly taken these steps pointed out by the Apostle Paul, then what? From there on we are persuaded that the knowledge of His will will come quite easily. If you have conscientiously taken those steps and are living at the very summit of the third one, (in fellowship with the Lord) there are at least *three infallible sources of divine guidance* which will supply and shed light on your path and direct you in the very center of God's will. The first of these sources of guidance is the *Word of God in the Holy Scriptures*.

1

The way to employ the Word of God as a source of divine guidance in your life is to *saturate yourself with*

74

that Word. God has to a large degree revealed His general mind and will for His children in the Bible. As men read the Scriptures, search the Scriptures, live in the Scriptures, they will learn the principles of divine guidance and glean much light for their own path. "No one can know all the will of God today without a knowledge of the Book." The Bible is the inerrant, infallible, eternal Word of God, the perfect revelation of the divine mind and heart of God, and of His general will for His children throughout the earth. So to the one who earnestly desires to know and to do God's will, we say, "Search the Scriptures." Saturate your heart and mind with the Scriptures. Meditate day and night in the Scriptures. Thus you shall be like the tree planted beside the rivers of water that bringeth forth fruit in its season, and whose leaf shall not wither. In other words, you shall derive from the Scriptures that general knowledge of God's will which is essential to a divinely-guided and fruitful Christian life.

Some people hold the mistaken view that certain parts of the Bible are of little importance and have no practical value upon the Christian's path today. This is erroneous. Every earnest Christian seeking divine guidance should read the whole Word of God, from cover to cover, at least once each year. It is impossible to overemphasize this point. In my own experience I have found that the more constantly I read the Word of God and search it the less perplexity I experience concerning His will. And this is the testimony of every servant of Christ. One man has made this rather striking statement, "When one is fully acquainted with the truths of Scripture, it seems that he, to a large degree, will just *automatically* understand the will of God."

From our own experience we can say amen to this statement. The Word of God should be in our hearts, and at our fingertips, and on our tongue's end. We should live in the Book, love it, memorize it, ruminate over it, feed upon it.

Every moment of spare time should be spent reading the Word of God and studying it. Abraham Lincoln testified to the value and profitableness of reading the Bible, even for light and guidance as a Statesman. And doubtless it was his full acquaintance with the Word of God and his constant perusal of it that gave him the special wisdom and guidance required of the President of the United States during that critical period of our history. And because we had in the White House a man who was thus guided by the Word of God, the whole history of our nation, and of other nations too, was molded. What if we had had an infidel President at that time, one who cared nothing for the Word of God? How different everything might have been! As one saturates his soul with the Bible it becomes a lamp to his feet and a light to his pathway, as the Psalmist said, (Psalm 119:105). In Hebrews 4:12 we are told that the Word of God is a "discerner of the thoughts and intents of the heart." How it does search and purge all our intents and motives! So if you really desire to know God's will, make the Word of God your constant companion. Know it better than you know anything else in this whole world.

2

The second way to employ the Bible as a source of divine guidance, is to *examine your prospects and plans in the light of it.* The primary question to ask, in seeking to know God's will, is, do the Scriptures throw any light on the thing that I am contemplating? Is this thing in harmony with the Word?

Sometimes young people come to me, with a certain kind of troubled look on their faces, with the request that I pray with them concerning how to know the will of God in relation to a certain vital question in their lives. Often when I think I can discern the nature of their question, I probe a little further and ask them to state exactly what their problem is. Then so often it comes out. They are in love with, or even engaged to, an unsaved person, and now want me to pray that God will manifest His will as to whether or not they should be married. In such a case there is nothing to pray about! It is contrary to the Word of God for the Christian to marry an unsaved one. We are exhorted to "Be not equally yoked together with unbelievers" (II Cor. 6:14). In the light of this same Scripture, it cannot be God's will for a Christian to enter into any other kind of binding association with an unbeliever, such as a business partnership, either. It is vain, and even wrong, to ask God for special guidance on problems to which the answers are clearly taught in the Scriptures. There is nothing to pray about. Such matters are settled and they ought to be understood as a matter of course.

Hence, by using the Scriptures in this way, *through the process of elimination,* the Christian comes to know God's will. God's Word may rightly be called our supreme source of guidance. Wherever it speaks plainly on any question, the man of God needs seek no further; its authority is final.

Of course the Bible could not contain detailed instructions for the individual life of every Christian. Such a volume, if it existed, would not be practical. So what about those questions upon which the Scriptures are silent? The Bible does not say, for instance, whether I should be a missionary, a pastor, a schoolteacher, a nurse, a businessman, or a farmer. How then can one find out from the Word which of these places my life is to fill? Let me say this: it is safe and right to pray for divine guidance in things upon which the Bible is silent—both in direct statement and by doctrinal implication. While the Bible is *one* of the sources of divine guidance, it is not the only one, as we shall see later. But taking the question as to whether one should be a missionary, be it plainly said, there is nothing so completely in harmony with the Scriptures as that. *The Bible sets forth the missionary program as a vital part of the plan of redemption.* The Book is full of it from cover to cover. The evangelizing of the world is as much a part of redemption's program as the death and resurrection of Jesus Christ! So you do not have to fear that your being a missionary is not in harmony with the Scripture. It is more in harmony with the Scripture than anything you could possibly do. Although the Bible contains specific instruction in missions, it has no definite instructions regarding the secular services which we have enumerated.

Sometimes young people seem fearful about going into missionary work lest it should be contrary to the will of God, then they turn around and enter into any kind of profession they themselves choose, without a single thought as to whether it is God's will or not for them to enter that particular profession. Is that a fair way to deal with God? Is it even a fair way to deal with one's self? It would seem that *there is more danger of getting out of the will of God by entering secular work than spiritual service,* for the Bible not only authorizes us to go and preach the Gospel but *commands* us to do so. The full plan of redemption as revealed in the Scriptures has not been carried out, and will not be carried out until the Gospel has been carried to every unreached part of the earth.

To sum this up pointedly, if you think you have a leading to do something which is contrary to written Scripture, be sure that leading is not of God. If you believe you have a leading to be a missionary, you may rest assured that that is in accordance with the Word of God. If you feel led to enter into some such service upon which the Scriptures are utterly silent, it is safe to assume that it *could* be God's will for you.

3

Another way to use the Bible as a source of guidance is to *ask and allow the Holy Spirit to direct you to certain specific verses and passages for direct leading.*

This is a point upon which questions are often raised. Is it safe to follow the leading of simply opening the Bible at random and allowing your eye to be fastened upon some certain verse or sentence? I believe the answer to that question depends entirely upon the spiritual life back of the act. If one is really walking in close communion with God, as we pointed out in Chapter IX, I believe the Holy Spirit can and does lead people in that way. But if one is living a careless and cold spiritual life he cannot just open the Bible at random under the pressure of some emergency, and expect the first Scripture his eyes light upon to be God's direction for his life. When the life is truly spiritual, and when one has earnestly implored God for guidance, and then prayerfully opens the Book in that manner, we believe he may thus be guided. In the same manner that the Spirit of God brings to a Christian heart messages of promise, comfort and assurance, in time of particular need, through specific passages of the Scripture, we believe He may also direct a truly spiritual heart into the will of God in the same manner. We do not however believe it is safe or right for a Christian to expect the over-all guidance of his entire life to be based upon this method. We rather consider it the unusual method, and also an elementary one; it is more the Spirit's method of dealing with babes in Christ than with mature spiritual men.

In closing this chapter we quote from the Psalmist who said, "The entrance of Thy Word giveth light." He doubtless meant that the entrance of God's Word into the human heart sheds light upon that life and upon life's pathway. Surely the saints of God of all the ages would testify that God's Word has been one of His supreme means of guiding His people.

There can never be any guidance contrary to the Word; there will seldom be guidance apart from the Word. Divine guidance must either come through, or in perfect harmony with, the written Word of God. Anything else is not divine guidance.

11

SOURCES OF GUIDANCE (Cont.)

THE WITNESS OF THE SPIRIT

VERY OFTEN we quote and hear quoted that passage of Scripture in Romans 8:16: "The Spirit himself beareth witness with our spirit that we are the children of God." But there is another verse almost directly before this one which is often overlooked. That is the 14th verse. It reads, "For as many as are led by the Spirit of God they are the sons of God." This verse indicates that to be Spirit-led is one of the evidences of divine sonship. It also naturally implies that all the children of God are led by the Spirit of God. As we put verse 14 and verse 16 together we find the two ways in which the Holy Spirit gives evidence that a man is a Christian—first, by directing his life; second, by bearing inward witness of personal assurance to his heart.

In the same manner that the Holy Spirit bears witness that we are the children of God He also bears witness to our hearts when we are walking in the will of God. One of His very purposes, according to the Scriptures, in taking up His abode in the Christian's life, is that He might be our Guide and Captain. As we study the work of the Holy Spirit in the hearts of the believers in the New Testament Scriptures, and in the Old Testament, too, for that matter, we will find that there are three outstanding ministries which He is to perform in us: He sanctifies, He empowers, and He enlightens. In giving the promise of the Spirit's coming the Saviour said to His disciples that night in the upper room, "I will not leave you comfortless" (John 14:18). The literal Greek rendering of this is, "I will not leave you orphans." An orphan is a child who has been left without parents. He has no one to look after him, to care for him, and to teach him and guide him in the ways of life. He is left without a caretaker or guide. The Lord Jesus Christ promised that He would not leave His people without a guide, like orphaned children, but would send the Holy Spirit to be to them their very father and guardian.

In the book of Acts one sees the guiding hand of the Holy Spirit in vivid operation in the early church. Let us briefly study some of these cases. In the eighth chapter we read, "And the angel of the Lord spake unto Philip, saying, Arise, and go toward the south unto the way that goeth down from Jerusalem unto Gaza . . . Then the Spirit said unto Philip, Go near, and join thyself to this chariot" (vv. 26, 29). Here is an example of leading by the Spirit of God, clear and direct. The Spirit clearly and specifically directed Philip to approach the chariot in which the Ethiopian was riding, and lead him to Christ.

In Acts 11:12 we have an even more outstanding case of the Spirit's guidance. Here Peter is relating to the church his experience in the house of Cornelius, and says, "And the Spirit bade me go with them, nothing doubting." In order to justify himself for going to the house of an uncircumcised man and mingling with such people and preaching the Gospel to them, Peter simply stated that it was the Holy Spirit who had led him to go with the men to Cornelius' house. In the preceding chapter, verse 19, we read the verification to this, "While Peter thought on the vision, the Spirit said unto him, behold, three men seek thee. Arise therefore, and get thee down, and go with them, doubting nothing; for I have sent them."

But the particular instance of the Spirit's guidance in this Book that stirs my own heart above all others, is in the 13th chapter. We read there, in verse 2, of the church at Antioch, "As they ministered to the Lord, and fasted, the Holy Ghost said, Separate me Barnabas and Saul for the work whereunto I have called them." Here is the inauguration of the great foreign missionary program of the church. How it thrills one's heart to read that it was the direct leading of the Holy Spirit that thrust forth Barnabas and Saul for that work. It was He who led the church at Antioch, and the two servants he had specifically chosen, to go forth on this first missionary tour. The Holy Spirit is Himself the Lord of the harvest, and one of His great missions in the world is to direct God's people in the carrying on of the great program of world evangelization as commanded by Christ our Saviour. If only Christians today lived as close to God as did the members of the early church and were as fully yielded to God, there would no doubt be many more who would hear the Holy Spirit calling them into particular fields and to specific tasks!

The illustration of a certain little girl may help us

here. A mother had told her daughter, after their evening meal that she was not to leave their own yard. The mother wanted her on hand so she could help her with some of the evening work later. When the time came for that service to be rendered, the mother called from both the back and the front door for the daughter to come and help her. There was no response. Later on, when the little girl came home, her mother chastened her for not coming when she was called. The little girl retaliated, "But, Mama, I didn't hear you call." "Well, if you had been in our own yard, near the house, as you were supposed to be, you would have heard when I called," was the mother's reply. I wonder if it is not often this way with Christians? They are too far away to hear the call of the Spirit. That is to say, they are not living in that close communion with Him that makes it possible for them to hear His voice when He seeks to make known to them God's will and plan for their lives.

The question may be asked, How does the Holy Spirit speak to us? How does He make known the will of God to us? Not necessarily, not usually, by a voice audible to our physical ears. There are other ears than our physical ones, even as there are other eyes than our physical ones. Sometimes in explaining the simple things of everyday life to another person we say, "Do you see?" Now of course we do not mean physical seeing, but rather mental comprehension. So also there are ears in our hearts to which the Holy Spirit can speak. In other words, the Holy Spirit reveals God's will to us by making certain indelible and inescapable impressions upon our minds and hearts that God wants us to do a certain thing. If we live close to Him in daily experience, and are sensitive to His impressions, He will be able to make known to us, clearly and exactly, what God's will is.

But another question arises! How can one discern between his own emotional impressions and the ones that come from the Spirit? How can one discern between his own feelings and the Spirit's witness? This we acknowledge and understand to be a real problem. But we believe there is help at this point also, that it is possible to know one from the other. Emotions are merely passing sentiments, or moods. They come and they go. It is a good thing we have emotions. They often relieve our feelings and make life interesting. Life would be very drab if there were no such thing as laughter. Life would also be very empty and shallow if there were no such thing as weeping. Some even call love an emotion, though this seems shallow. What would a life be like that never knew or experienced love? But our emotional feelings and experiences are so vascillating. They do not abide. They are not permanent. It is good to laugh at times, but who likes to be around a person who laughs and giggles incessantly? It is good at times to weep. But who likes to be around a person who is always weeping and whining? It is well for people to become hilarious on certain occasions, but who likes to be around a person who is up in the clouds all the time, or one who is always down in the valley of despair?

It is at this point that we can discern the difference between our own emotional impressions and those impressions inscribed on our hearts by the Holy Spirit. The impressions of the Spirit are impressions which remain. They are there today, tomorrow, next week, next month and still next year. They do not just come and then go. A Christian young man hears a missionary from Africa, his emotions are all stirred up, and immediately he thinks he should go to Africa. He hears someone else from China and has the same reaction—then another from South America, with still the same reaction. Obviously those impressions were not from the Holy Spirit, for the Holy Spirit would not change His mind with the different speakers. No, when the Spirit of God lays a certain field of the world upon one's heart, no matter what comes, he cannot get away from the impression that *there* is God's field of service for him. That kind of impression may rightly be understood to be the voice of the Spirit speaking. When the time comes for a Christian, who is prepared and fitted for God's service, to know God's exact place of service for him, the Holy Spirit will lay a definite work or field upon that person's heart with an indelible and unshaken impression that he cannot get away from. That is the way He speaks.

The Spirit not only directs the course and work of one's entire life, but He also guides the Christian from day to day in particular instances and special services which God's will has for him along life's path. The experience of a missionary in the jungles of inner South America illustrates this very well. It is a gripping and striking account. On a particular morning this missionary received the distinct impression that he should make a trip in a certain direction into the surrounding jungles that very day. When he made a trip into the jungles, he usually prepared for it several days in advance, so at first he merely ignored this impression, considering it only his personal "feeling." As the morning wore on, he could not be rid of the impression that he must go to that particular area without delay. He quickly got together some things for the journey, called a few of his Indian carriers, and set out. After long, weary trekking through the dense jungles, they arrived at nightfall at an Indian hut. Inside the bamboo hut was an old Indian man, literally on his deathbed. Strange to say, he seemed all prepared for the missionary's coming and almost immediately asked about "The Book." Upon the missionary's inquiry, the aged, dying pagan related how the preceding night, after he had cried out to God for hope and light in his darkness, he had had a dream wherein a messenger came to him from heaven bringing a book. He was told to believe the words and message of the Book, and he would thus be saved. But the dream was soon over, and there he lay again in his hut in heathen darkness. Now the white man had come with the Book. He would believe and be saved! To make a long story short, the old Indian put his trust in Christ and shortly passed away to be with his Lord.

In such an experience one sees the Spirit's special leading in a particular event. He spoke to the heart of the missionary and guided him to the hut of the benighted man. He also spoke, in another manner, to an earnest heathen who was seeking light and prepared him for the message of the gospel that was going to be brought to him. Any saint who has obeyed the voice of the Holy Spirit calling him into the will of God for his life may expect such experiences as this along his pathway. The life that has followed over-all guidance can expect particular guidance.

Holy Spirit, faithful Guide,
Ever near the Christian's side;
Gently lead us by the hand,
Pilgrims in a desert land;
Weary souls fore'er rejoice,
While they hear that sweetest voice,
Whisp'ring softly, "Wand'rer, come.
Follow Me, I'll guide thee home."

Ever present, truest Friend,
Ever near Thine aid to lend,
Leave us not to doubt and fear,
Groping on in darkness drear;
When the storms are raging sore,
Hearts grow faint, and hopes give o'er,
Whisper softly, "Wand'rer, come!
Follow Me, I'll guide thee home."

When our days of toil shall cease,
Waiting still for sweet release,
Nothing left but Heav'n and prayer,
Wond'ring if our names were there;
Wading deep the dismal flood,
Pleading naught but Jesus' blood,
Whisper softly, "Wand'rer come!
Follow Me, I'll guide thee home."

Has the Spirit borne witness that you are to do a certain work for God? As you heed that impression and pray over it, does it become deeper and more indelible on your heart? As you yield toward the carrying out of that impression does there come a deep and settled peace to your soul? If so, it is doubtless the leading of the Holy Spirit. This, however, brings the question we raised at first: Have you yielded your life completely to the Holy Spirit? As you know your own heart, have you utterly yielded yourself to God? Has there been a time in your life when you came to the place where it became your fixed intention to surrender everything to the will and working of the Spirit? One missionary has put it, "Such a surrender is not easy, nor as complete as we oftentimes suppose. Yet, is it right to expect God to lead you to the field of *His* choice if you have already determined in your own heart where *you* want to go? If you really want His guidance, you have to be ready to put yourself in His hands and gladly follow His directions, *wherever they may lead.* Does selfish ambition enter into your plans, the desire for recognition and praise from other Christians? It is better, and infinitely more satisfying, to please God than men."

12

SOURCES OF GUIDANCE (Cont.)

THE WORKS OF PROVIDENCE

THE SAINTED GEORGE MUELLER, whose faith God so marvelously honored and of whom we shall say more in the next chapter, said this with reference to divine guidance: "I take into account providential circumstances. These often plainly indicate God's will in connection with His Word and Spirit."

Many a saint of God testified that God has directed him into the divine will by working the circumstances of his life to that end. One servant of Christ put it thus: "He buttresses the inner guidance by external circumstances . . . He forges one link after another in the chain of guidance until the whole is complete and convincing." The royal chain of God's divine plan for your life and mine is woven out of the single links which we lay hold of, one at a time, along the pathway of daily duty. After we have gathered enough of the links, the chain itself makes its appearance. The man who faithfully and prayerfully picks up the links formed in the forge of life's circumstances need never fear missing the entire golden chain.

We wish to give at least two examples of guidance by circumstances from the Scriptures—one from the Old Testament and one from the New. First, let us go to the 45th chapter of the Book of Genesis, to the life of Joseph. What a chain of circumstances, over which Joseph had no personal control, was wrought by the Divine Hand to guide the life of this servant of His! And some of these very circumstances which made up the "royal row of guidance" in his life came from evil hearts and evil hands. Yet Jehovah overruled it all, and through that chain of circumstances guided the life of His chosen one. Read verses five to fifteen of Genesis forty-five in your Bible. Note what Joseph says, beginning at verse five, "Now therefore be not grieved, not angry with yourselves, that ye sold me hither: *for God did send me before you to preserve life* . . . And God sent me before you to preserve you a posterity in the earth, and to save your lives by a great deliverance. So *now it was not you that sent me hither, but God:* and He hath made me a father to Pharaoh, and lord of all his house, and a ruler throughout all the land of Egypt." Doubtless it was hard for Joseph to see how God was molding and leading his life through some of the bitter circumstances that had come to him during the time he was passing through them, but now as he looks back over that divine chain he does so with real joy and confidence. Or, perhaps Joseph, who doubtless lived a life of true fellowship with the Lord, knew all the time that God's Hand was guiding him in those circumstances. However that may have been, God's Hand *was guiding*.

Another outstanding example of guidance by circumstances is found in the sixteenth chapter of Acts, verse seven. We read there, "After they were come to Mysia, they assayed to go into Bithynia: but the Spirit suffered them not." Here stands the great missionary and Apostle, Paul, and his missionary companions. They were endeavoring to enter a field to which God was not leading them, so "the Spirit suffered them not." We are not told how the Spirit hindered them from entering into Mysia, but it is commonly understood by Bible commentators that the doors were closed into that area. Note also verse six of the same chapter, "Now when they had gone throughout Phyrgia and the region of Galatia, and were *forbidden of the Holy Ghost to* preach the word in Asia. . . . " This evidently was the same situation. There evidently was some circumstance which prohibited the Apostle Paul and his colleagues from entering Asia Minor and from preaching the gospel there. Notice, first they endeavored to go to the left hand, then they endeavored to go to the right hand and were similarly hindered, yet all the time it was the Hand of God guiding through those hindering circumstances. God was leading them on to Philippi. Later, when they came to Troas, straight on ahead, there appeared to Paul a vision of the man of Macedonia saying, "Come over into Macedonia and help us." So here is a clear case of guidance through circumstances, and also by direct call from the Holy Spirit; a combination of leading through natural circumstances and a supernatural call. Doors were closed on the right hand and on the left, hence the missionaries proceeded to Troas. At Troas, as another link in the chain of guidance, God's Spirit spoke to them.

Even the great Apostle Paul, who certainly knew what it meant to follow the Lord, twice could have, and apparently would have, gone the wrong direction had not circumstances hindered him. Let us not forget that behind all the circumstances of the Christian's life there is the all-powerful, all-wise Hand of our Heavenly Father at work. That hand shapes and molds the circumstances of our lives, in order that our lives might be fashioned and shaped to know and to fit into His will.

We can learn from this incident that *stops* of a good man, as well as his *steps,* are ordered by the Lord. When you drive through traffic in a modern city it is an obvious fact that the "stop-lights" guide you as much as the "go-lights" do. That is sometimes hard for God's people to understand. When we are hindered from going forward we are prone to think we are not having guidance. In fact no guidance forward may be guidance of the most definite kind. It may be *guidance to wait.* Waiting, with the guiding cloud, is just as true a guidance as going forward. It is much safer to wait with God than to go forward simply in human willfulness. Very often God's guidance is shown by closed doors.

Sometimes guidance through circumstances is plain and easy to discern. At other times it may not be so easy, and we need to bear in mind that we have to depend upon the Holy Spirit to interpret circumstances. It is not likely, for instance, that God would want a blind man, or an invalid, or a cripple, to go to the foreign field as a missionary. The circumstances of his life serve as guidance from God that the foreign field is not his place. Or, if you as a Christian young person should be the sole support of invalid parents it is quite clear that God would not want you to leave them and go to Africa (I Tim. 5:8). Or, if you are efficient and natural in the business world, and a complete failure as a speaker or platform man, it is quite apparent that God is not calling you into the work of a pastor. Neither would an unlearned man be led on the mission field to translation work which required educated talent.

To bring this right down to earth, if you have an impression in your heart which you have interpreted to be the witness of the Spirit leading you, move in that direction. If perchance you have been mistaken, it is God's business to close the doors in the way of its accomplishment. Suppose for instance, you felt led to the mission field and already had applied to a Mission Board, and were accepted, and yet this was not God's place for you. Then what? God can easily bring some circumstance to pass that will absolutely close the door in your face. And He would do just that too, in the life of any conscientious Christian *earnestly seeking* to know and follow His will.

Some of the world's outstanding missionaries were guided to their fields by circumstances, some of them rather peculiar ones. David Livingstone, the well-known missionary to Africa, shortly after his conversion became interested in missions, because, as he said, "The salvation of men ought to be the chief desire and aim of every Christian." But the decision to give his own life to missionary work came as a result of his reading an appeal by Dr. Carl Gutzlaff, a missionary to China. Livingstone offered himself to go to China and arranged for medical training in anticipation of service in that land. But, when he was ready to go the doors to China were closed because of the terrible opium war. The London Missionary Society then wanted to send him to the West Indies, but he protested that his medical knowledge would not be called into use there, since they already had doctors in that area. Finally, as a result of his contacts with Robert Moffat, the pioneer missionary to South Africa, Livingstone's heart was turned to Africa. Who, reading Livingstone's life today, could doubt that he found the will of God for his life?

Adoniram Judson, the early American pioneer to the Far East, was also remarkably led through circumstances. At the age of twenty-one Judson read a printed sermon by Claudius Buchanan of England, who had served as a Chaplain of the British East India Company in India for a good many years. It told how God's power was being manifest in India, and dwelt particularly on the extensive and fruitful labors of the German missionary, Frederick Swartz, sent out by the Halle Mission. As someone else put it, "This sermon fell like a spark on the tinder of Judson's soul," and six months later he made his decision to become a missionary. He really started out for India when he set sail, but when he arrived he was not permitted to land, so he got off at the next place where the ship docked—namely, Rangoon, Burma. In the country of Burma he spent his life, and did a work for God which makes it unquestioned that God had called him to that land to preach the Gospel—through providential circumstances.

John G. Paton, the heroic missionary to the New Hebrides Islands of the South Pacific, began his Christian service as a city missionary in his native land of Scotland. "Happy in my work as I felt," he wrote, "and successful by the blessing of God, yet I continually heard . . . the wail of the perishing heathen in the South Seas; and I saw that few were caring for them, while I well knew that many would be ready to take up my work in Calton and carry it forward, perhaps with more efficiency than myself." The Presbyterian Church to which he belonged had been seeking for a missionary for two years to join John Inglis in the work in the New Hebrides, but no one had offered to go. Though John Paton was anxious to offer himself, so that he could hardly overpower the impulse to get up in a meeting and answer aloud, "Here am I, send me," he was very much·afraid of mistaking his own impressions for the voice of the Holy Spirit. He continued to meditate and pray, but was increasingly impressed that God was calling him to the foreign field. He saw the spiritual plight of the heathen Islanders and saw by contrast how readily available were the means of grace in Scotland. Finally he said, "From every aspect at which I could *look the facts in the face,* the voice within me sounded like a *voice from God."* And upon that conviction and leading he went forth! Who could doubt that *he found God's will?* Who could doubt that he *did* God's will?

Also helpful to note was the way John Scudder, the first American medical missionary to India, heard the call of God. At the insistence of his father he had received medical training and established a fine practice here in the homeland, though his own youthful desire had been to be a minister. While visiting a Christian patient, he came across the tract, *The Claims of Six Hundred Millions,* which he borrowed from the lady to read. After reading it over and over again, he fell on his knees before God, and asked, "Lord, what wilt Thou have me to do?" The still, small voice seemed to say clearly, "Go and preach the Gospel to the heathen." Scudder was ready to obey and told the Lord so. But what about his wife? He could not go without taking her, nor would he take her against her will. So he prayfully decided, as he himself put it, to "lay the matter before *her* mind as it lays before mine. If she says nay, I shall regard it as settling the question." However, Mrs. Scudder *was ready* to go with him to the mission field, and not long after that, when the American Board sent out an appeal for a missionary doctor for India, they offered themselves and were sent out. Who that has read about the life of John Scudder could doubt that his guidance was from God?

Yes, God has guided and still does guide His own through common circumstances of daily life. But we need to be sure that we, by a close fellowship with the Spirit, properly interpret the circumstances and discern the mind of God in them, for circumstances in themselves are not an infallible guide. Philip, the Evangelist, was called to leave a great revival to minister to one lone soul on a desert road (Acts 8:5, 26). That surely was contrary to the leading of circumstances. God called the uneducated, unpolished, poorly talented Dwight L. Moody, from selling shoes in a Boston shoe shop, to go to the evangelistic platform as a preacher to multitudes on both sides of the Atlantic and to become a winner of thousands.

May we submit an illustration to show how, when God is leading, all these three sources of guidance correspond and dovetail together? F. B. Meyer was once asked by a certain Christian how a person might unmistakably recognize the will of God. His reply was: "This question was answered for me once on board ship, as in a very dark night we were entering harbor. I asked the captain how he was able to find the narrow entrance to the harbor at night. He said to me, 'See yonder three lights? When those lights are in correct alignment, I know I am in the right channel.' So it is with the will of God. When the Word of God, the impulse of the Holy Spirit in my heart, and the outward circumstances are in harmony, then I am convinced that I am acting in accordance with the will of God."

What about "putting out the fleece?" In other words, what about asking God for certain providential "signs" for assurance of His will, as Gideon did? (See Judges 6:36-40). Is this a legitimate and safe way to seek Divine Guidance?

Well, it seems safe to say that this is the most common method Christians can use in seeking God's will, in fact the only one many know anything about. In the case of Gideon, however, one ought to remember that God had already plainly appeared to him and told him what he was to do, and the matter of the fleece actually reflects doubt and fear on Gideon's part. Nevertheless, because Gideon was sincere, God met him on his two propositions.

Perhaps this "sign" method of ascertaining the will of the Lord has broken down in effectiveness with Christians today because many who have never really entered into the surrendered, Spirit-filled life, seek to use it. What we said earlier about guidance from specific verses of Scripture applies here also: carnal Christians cannot rely upon such guidance. Indeed, as I think we have amply demonstrated, carnal Christians cannot find God's will by *any* method or means. They are not fitted.

But, an earnest, surrendered, Spirit-filled Christian

may certainly ask God to reveal His will in a given matter by creating or changing certain circumstances. Make sure, however, when you pray thus, that you are absolutely honest with God and with yourself, and that your own will is entirely ruled out of the case. Don't ask God for some outlandish sign or circumstance to prove He wants you to do a certain thing when actually in your own heart there is unwillingness to do it, and a secret hope the special circumstance you requested will not come to pass. That is not being open and honest with the Lord. When you ask for a sign, be unbiased as Gideon was, for he asked God to produce a certain circumstance, and then the next morning to reverse it! This showed Gideon's sincerity and earnestness, and that was why God met his request. He will meet yours too when He sees you are as surrendered and sincere as Gideon.

To make it simple and as practical as possible, test, try, prove the will of God for your life, by asking yourself six vital questions, based on this and the preceding five chapters of our book: *First,* Have I utterly surrendered my will and life up to God as a living sacrifice, and is my heart so surrendered now in everything? *Second,* Have I renounced the world in every known form, and is my life now fully separated from it? *Third,* Have I been walking in true and close fellowship with God as I have contemplated this, and is my heart engaged in such fellowship at the present time? *Fourth,* Is this thing I am now contemplating according to the Word of God, or expedient in the light of the Word? *Fifth,* Has a deep impression been placed on my heart in this direction, which persists with the passing of time, and deepens within me as I pray and seek the

99

mind of God? *Sixth,* Do the circumstances that surround my life point in this same direction?

If these questions can honestly and earnestly be answered in the affirmative you may be assured of knowing the will of God.

13

MUELLER'S METHOD

GEORGE MUELLER, of Bristol, England, founder and director of a large children's orphanage, which he carried on by simple faith, to the amazement of the whole world, was one of the spiritual giants of the preceding century. During the course of his lifetime $7,500,000 was entrusted to him and was spent for the care and maintenance of thousands of orphaned children, in response to prayer, without any form of solicitation. (On today's scale this would be the equivalent of $25,000,000).

The story of Mueller's life and faith and the marvelous answers to prayer which he experienced is indeed a spiritual romance. He became the Christian world's great example of the life of faith, and his orphanage work became the outstanding monument to the work of faith. All the money that came into his hands, and all the marvelous and detailed guidance which he received from God came in response to earnest prayer and a simple, childlike faith.

Here is Mueller's simple formula for determining the divine will, as he himself gave it:

How I Ascertain the Will of God

"1. I seek at the beginning to get my heart into such a state that it has no will of its own in regard to a given matter.

"Nine-tenths of the trouble with people is just here. Nine-tenths of the difficulties are overcome when our hearts are ready to do the Lord's will, whatever it may be. When one is truly in this state, it is usually but a little way to the knowledge of what His will is.

"2. Having done this, I do not leave the result to feeling or single impression. If I do so, I make myself liable to great delusions.

"3. I seek the will of the Spirit of God through, or in connection with, the Word of God. The Spirit and the Word must be combined. If I look to the Spirit alone without the Word, I lay myself open to great delusions also. If the Holy Ghost guides us at all, He will do it according to the Scriptures and never contrary to them.

"4. Next I take into account providential circumstances. These often plainly indicate God's will in connection with His Word and Spirit.

"5. I ask God in prayer to reveal His will to me aright.

"6. Thus, through prayer, the study of the Word, and reflection, I come to a deliberate judgment according to the best of my ability and knowledge, and if my mind is thus at peace and continues so after two or three more petitions, I proceed accordingly.

"In trivial matters and in transactions involving most important issues I have found this method always effective."

Someone has boiled Mueller's formula, if we may rightly call it that, down to the following:

1. Surrender your own will.
2. Seek the Spirit's will through God's Word.
3. Note providential circumstances.
4. Pray for guidance.
5. Wait on God.

But, though Mr. Mueller thus expressed on paper briefly how he set about to determine the mind and will of God in specific matters, there was more to his actual practice than might appear from so simple a statement. For in his journal he has written that on many occasions, when momentous decisions faced him, he would shut himself up in his room for long sessions before the Lord, examining his own heart in the Divine Presence and calling on the Heavenly Father for wisdom and light. Then after spending ample time in heart-searching and prayer, he calmly and deliberately took a blank sheet of paper and drew a line down the center. On one side of the line he listed all the factors he could think of which were in favor of the proposition which he was facing, and on the other side he listed all the factors which were against it. This he called his "balance sheet." Over this balance sheet he prayerfully meditated for several days, revising the list from day to day as seemed necessary, by adding contributing or opposing factors that occurred to him. Sooner or later the result was that there was borne upon his heart a definite conviction regarding the matter as to what course he should follow. If the conviction thus borne upon him continued and became intensified, after further definite committal to God, he proceeded along the line which he felt to be God's indicated will.

Other Christians have used this "balance sheet" method in finding out God's will. But we caution you, reader, that only those who live prayerful, devoted, and godly lives, can use it successfully. If a carnal Christian, who has never come up the steps of Romans 12:1, 2, seeks to use it the decision he arrives at will be merely a human and intellectual one, and there can be no genuine certainty that he has found the will of God. Not only does this method demand utter surrender, sanctification, and walking in the Spirit, but also absolute honesty with one's self and with God in one's thinking. As Mr. Mueller practiced the balance sheet method, never once did he find the leading he thus received to be in error. And, if we live as godly and faithful a life as Mueller did, it will work the same way with us.

Mr. Downing, whom we quoted earlier, has the following to say regarding this method of guidance: "The simple suggestion made years ago to a group of Bible students by the General Director of our mission (Africa Inland Mission), will I hope prove as helpful to you as it has been to me.

"When desirous of knowing God's will concerning an important matter, especially if it be whether or not you should do a particular thing, draw a line through a blank sheet of paper, and on one side write all the reasons for, and on the other side, all the reasons against doing the thing. Pray over these reasons. If necessary revise the list from day to day while alone with Him at the appointed time. Ere long quite a distinct impression will be borne in upon your heart in favor of one side or the other. If the impression which comes today is from the Spirit of God, it will be deeper tomorrow; if not from Him, it will fade out. We should,

I believe, regard as from the Lord the impressions that come to us when we are alone with Him and absolutely yielded, i.e. perfectly willing to do or not to do the thing about which we are inquiring. . . . It is easy to become presumptuous and fanatical, but let us remember that we are in God's school, pupils to be taught individually by His Spirit, then seek to discover His method of influencing us personally. I am not emotional; I do not have visions or such spectacular experiences as I have heard others relate. In my experience the leading comes through gradually deepening inward impressions."

For want of a more appropriate place to do so, we shall insert in this chapter some comments on a subject that has already been alluded to but needs further emphasis. That is that a layman may be in God's will as much as a missionary or minister. We must not misunderstand this. We realize that much of what we have written in this book is designed for those whom God desires to call into definite full-time Christian service, and we acknowledge further that much of this has been from a heart burdened for the regions beyond, where more than a thousand million souls sit today in darkness, despair, and death. But even such a burden must not be allowed to obscure the fact that God needs laymen as well as missionaries and ministers, and He calls such just as definitely.

Often when you talk about the will of God and consecration, Christian men immediately get the idea that they must give up their business and start for the pulpit or the mission field. Willingness to devote one's full life to the direct ministry of the Gospel is important, but certainly it is not absolutely decisive or all-inclusive. There is a location in God's vineyard which can be determined only by the Lord Himself. God needs laborers and businessmen to earn money to give for support of those who enter the fields of service, and missionary work, as well as He needs men to enter them. All cannot devote their full time to preaching. Neither can all devote their lives to industry and business. Some must do one, some the other; and all is to be subject to the Master's will. To be surrendered to God means that I must be as ready to do one as the other. Is that *your* attitude today, reader? Remember, the leading of God is as important in the one direction as it is in the other.

Too often God's people automatically suppose that to enter into God's plan for their lives demands that they go to some *other place*. This is not necessarily so. In fact, there is danger of making a grave mistake at this very point. Consecration does not necessarily involve *dis-location*. Oftentimes it is not a new sphere God is seeking for the man, but rather a new man in the present sphere! It may not be *transportation* that is demanded by the divine will, but rather *transformation*. You cannot be completely yielded to, or completely right with God, unless you are willing either to go to the mission field or stay home and work and earn money to give so another can go, just as He may desire. God's people must be ready to do anything; who shall do which is for God Himself to decide and reveal.

We cannot close this chapter without quoting again from James McConkey: "Sometimes our perplexity is so great that it seems no guidance will ever come. For such times the psalmist has a precious message in his word about the night-watchers. 'My soul waiteth for the

Lord more than they that watch for the morning.' (Ps. 130:6.) How do men who wait in the night hours for the dawn, watch for the morning? The answer is fourfold:

"They watch in *darkness.*

"They watch for that which *comes slowly.*

"They watch for that which is *sure to come.*

"They watch for that which when it does come *brings the light of day.*

"So it is with us who wait for guidance. Often our perplexity is so extreme that we seem to be waiting in total darkness. Often too as we wait, even as those who wait for the day, the first faint streaks of dawn seem to come, *oh, so slowly!* Then too, as there never yet has been a night which was not *sure* to end in the dawn, so our night of uncertainty is sure to end in the dawning light of God's guidance. Lastly, as the slow-coming dawn, when it does arrive, brings light and blessing without measure, so when our God-given guidance at last breaks upon us it will so gladden our waiting souls and so illumine our beclouded path we shall almost forget the long days when we waited in darkness."

14

*THE MISSIONARY CALL

WE COME NOW to the vital question of the Missionary Call. The writer has been aware of his need of guidance from the Spirit of God all through these pages, sensing keenly the importance of the task undertaken, but especially as he comes to this special part does he realize his need of divine assistance.

There is much disagreement concerning the missionary call, even outright controversy, which has led to widespread confusion among Christian young people. Some men, including missionaries themselves, insist that no specific call is needed to the mission field. They point out that we have the command of Christ to "Go into all the world and preach the Gospel to every creature," and that since this has not yet been completed, the command and the need constitute the only call one

---

* The contents of this chapter were originally given in a missionary message by the author in the Annual Missionary Conference of the Scofield Memorial Church, Dallas, Texas, on Sunday, March 6, 1949. It was repeated before Southeastern Regional Fall Conference of the Inter-Varsity Christian Fellowship at Toccoa Falls, Georgia, and at some other missionary gatherings. Many young people were helped by the message, according to their testimonies. Ponder it with an open heart.

needs or should expect. They say all of us are called to the mission field and that if any specific call be required it should rather be to stay in the homeland. "Unless one can say he has been called to stay at home, he is called to go, in the light of the Great Commission—this statement is frequently made to young people. On the other hand, there are mission leaders and missionaries who stress the need of a specific personal call from God before anyone should go to a foreign field. They emphasize this strongly as they speak to young people, telling them that unless they can look back to a definite call when they get to the field and things go hard, they will not be able to stand the test and remain on the field.

Now suppose a missionary holding the first view comes to a church, or Christian school, emphasizing his idea; then the following week another missionary comes to address the same group, pressing home the latter view. I put myself in the place of those Christian young people and try to analyze their experience. What turmoil it must leave their souls in! What confusion of mind and heart they must inevitably have. Granting both these missionaries were sincere and seasoned Christian men, what must the reaction be in the hearts of their hearers?

As to the young folks themselves, some of them say they have never heard a call to the mission field, and hence contemplate no steps in that direction. Granting that some say this lightly and indifferently, there are unquestionably others who say it in all sincerity. They feel no sense of responsibility to the mission field because they have not been "called." Yet, that kind of attitude invariably causes one to experience a kind of spiritual "shudder;" there seems to be shallowness and coldness in it that in turn leaves one's own heart trembling and cold. On the other hand, as the Director of a Missionary Society, we have to confess a similar inward trembling and feeling of misgiving when interviewing a young person for the mission field who frankly states that the only call he has is found in the Scriptures and through the need of the fields. Where is the balance of truth in this great and important matter? Where is the right position? Where is that solid, sacred ground?

Is there not an answer to this problem? For surely a problem it is, and one too serious to be played with or passed by lightly. Is there not somewhere a point of reconciliation between these two opposite conceptions which represents the real truth of the matter? Is there not some additional light to be had on the whole question? We believe there is, and request our reader to pursue this chapter diligently to its end, and then carefully ponder its contents after this little book has been laid aside. We shall humbly seek to set forth the whole matter, embracing the respective truths on both sides of the question, and, by God's grace, lead the seeking young saint to the safe path of guidance:

1

There is, first of all, and unquestionably, *The Call That Comes from the Region Beyond* (2 Cor. 10:16).

It was this ceaseless call from "the regions beyond" that rang in the ears of the Apostle Paul all the days and years of his life, and ever drove him forward and onward in his missionary career. This call he both heard and heeded, being full of the Holy Ghost and full of the Holy *Go,* conditions which are inseparable in any life.

What do we mean by this call? What is its nature? It is precisely the same call with which Christ challenged his disciples in John 4:35, "Say not ye, there are yet four months, and then cometh the harvest. Behold, I say unto you, Lift up your eyes, and look on the fields; for they are white already to harvest." By the Call of The Region Beyond is meant *The Call of the Fields.* Do not ripened fields of grain, though possessing no articulate voice, *call for reapers?* Does not the ripened, falling grain, though "dumb" and speechless, call for harvesters? Most assuredly. No one who views the fields can fail to hear their call.

In the World-Wide Missionary Survey Conference held in Lansing, Michigan, and the surrounding area, in October, 1949, Ralph T. Davis, General Secretary of the Africa Inland Mission, speaking on this verse, contrasted *"The Saviour's Word,* 'Already' " with *"Man's World,* 'Yet,' " and then emphasized *"The Lord's Command,* 'Look'—Lift Up Your Eyes, transport your gaze from the things close around you, in your own immediate sphere of life, and look upon the fields of earth that are already overripe to harvest."

Do not the great unreached mission fields of the world in "the regions beyond," "beyond" our own borders, "beyond" the seas, call for spiritual reapers? Is this not then a missionary call? Perhaps in all the history of the church the fields have never been whiter or the opportunities larger than at this present hour. Is this not a call? Are not these whitened fields loudly calling to us, young men and women who know Christ?

Is not disillusioned Japan calling? Is not bleeding China calling? Is not awakened Latin America calling? Is not new Africa calling? Are not the great untouched areas of Central Asia calling? Are not the unreached lands of Islam calling? Who could deny it? And does not this call come to every Christian? Have you not heard missionaries pleading and praying for laborers to be sent to these harvests?

Is not this call from the regions beyond loud, definite, and clear? If you have answered this question as we feel you must, and already have, then it is apparently not right for you to say you have never heard a call. Surely all have heard, and are still hearing this call—*the call from the regions beyond.*

2

Secondly, there is *The Call That Comes from the Region Above.*

This of course is the call from heaven, where Christ sitteth on the right hand of God. Jesus Christ, our Risen, Exalted Saviour and Lord, the Great Head of the Church, is still calling for laborers for the unreached fields of earth. His last command to His disciples before "He was taken up, and a cloud received Him out of their sight" was "Ye shall be witnesses unto me . . . unto the uttermost part of the earth" (Acts 1:8). In Mark's Gospel the same Great Commission is stated in these plain words, "Go ye into all the world, and preach the Gospel to every creature." Has this command ever been withdrawn? Has this order at any time been rescinded? Has it ever been altered? Is the task completed, or is it still unfinished? Now, if Jesus issued this call to His

Church, if it has never been rescinded, and if the task has never been carried through to completion, then *the call still stands*. If He gave this command as He ascended to glory, surely He is still issuing it from His throne above.

The Lord Jesus, who gave the Great Commission to His people so long ago, is looking down upon the world and upon the Church from the battlements of heaven above, looking for men and women to perform His great mission of world-evangelization. He is looking down at us and asking, as He asked Isaiah of old, "Whom shall I send?" and then responds to His own question with "Who *will go* for me?" When Isaiah answered by saying, "Here am I, Lord, send me," He immediately said, "GO," (Isaiah 6:8,9). From heaven above, from the right hand of the throne of God, He is still calling, still commanding, still saying, "Go"— *"Go into all the world* and preach the Gospel to every creature." You say you have never heard any missionary call, young man, young woman? That cannot be wholly true, for surely you have heard this one. Look at it, face it squarely as it stands written in the Word, don't try to ignore it; *heed it* in the very depths of your soul, and ask Him what you are to do about it.

Christ died for all men (I John 2:2). He suffered for all (Isa. 53:6). He bore the sins of the entire world on the cross (John 1:29). He loves all. He longs for all to come to repentance (2 Pet. 3:9). He desires all to come to a knowledge of the Gospel, so that "whosoever will" may be saved. He placed the responsibility of this upon us as His people; He is still calling and pleading with us to hasten and tell them how they may be saved.

113

Some day we will stand before Him to give account of our lives (2 Cor. 5:10). We will surely have to give some kind of accounting regarding our relationship to the Great Commission, and what we did about it. Why did John speak of the possibility of Christians being ashamed before Him at His coming? (I John 2:28).

No, it is not possible to say, "I have heard the call." You have heard this call from the lips of Christ over and over again! And the call that sounded forth from the Saviour's lips on the Mount of Olives, still comes ringing in our ears from heaven above where He, as the Great Head of the Church, now has His place.

3

There is also *The Call That Comes from the Regions Below*.

This is a call that comes loud and clear, with an appeal that should verily rend the heart of every Christian young man and woman in our land. And yet it is one that few have noted or listened to. This call, perhaps "cry" would express it more truthfully, is echoed back to us from the region of Hades in the sixteenth chapter of the Gospel of Luke. "And it came to pass that the beggar died and was carried by the angels into Abraham's bosom: the rich man died also, and was buried; and in hades he lift up his eyes, being in torments . . . and he cried and said, Father Abraham, have mercy on me, . . . Then he said, I pray thee . . . that thou wouldest send him (Lazarus) to my father's house: *For I have five brethren; that he might testify*

114

unto them, lest they also come into this place of tor-ment" (vv. 22-28).

Here is a lost soul in Hades, in the regions below, crying out for someone to go to his people yet alive on earth to testify to them on the way of salvation that they may not come to the same hopeless fate. Note the pathos and appeal of this cry, *"Lest they also come into this place of torment!"* What a missionary call this is, one that should penetrate our souls to the quick and ring in our ears unremittingly. What a call, what a cry, what a request, what an appeal!

Who can read Luke 16 and say he has never heard a missionary call? Whose spiritual ears could be numb to such a call on this, echoed back to earth in the pages of Holy Writ from lost men and women in the bowels of Hades? If that *one soul* that Jesus tells about in this Scripture issued a call in behalf of *his* brethren and *his people,* have not the countless multitudes who have gone to join that host of the doomed issued forth a similar cry? Ah, yes, surely there are millions of souls down in Hades, hopeless and helpless, who cry end-lessly for some messenger of salvation to be sent to the ones they loved, to "testify unto them, lest they also come into this place of torment!" These know what it is to be lost, to be doomed, to be separated from God, to suffer the penalty of sin, and they cannot but plead and cry in behalf of their own.

You may say, "Do you mean to imply that the heathen are lost?" Friend, do you mean to imply that they are saved? Do you really think a soul can be saved without coming to Christ, who said, "I am the way, the truth, and the life: no man cometh unto the Father but by Me?" Can you believe that men who follow heathen religions, which everywhere in the Bible are regarded as Satanic in origin and operation, can thus get to heaven in the light of such divinely inspired statements as: "Neither is there salvation in any other: for there is none other name under heaven given among men, whereby we must be saved" (Acts 4:12); "This is the record, that God hath given us eternal life, and this life is in His Son. He that hath the Son hath life, and he that hath not the Son of God hath not life" (I John 5:11, 12); "Except a man be born again, He cannot see the kingdom of God" (John 3:3); and "At that time ye were without Christ . . . having no hope and without God in the world" (Eph. 2:12).

In a leaflet entitled "Are the Heathen Lost?" published by the Sudan Interior Mission, the Rev. Carl J. Tanis, after giving a strong collation of Scripture on the question, makes this statement, "Do you believe that the heathen will be saved and some day enter heaven without Christ? Surely *not!* If you believe that, then what proportion of them will be there and how will they be saved? They cannot have the imputed righteousness through faith in Christ, unless they know Him. They cannot have the actual righteousness made possible by the power of the Holy Spirit in the new birth, unless they believe on Christ. Romans 10:14 'How then shall they call on Him in whom they have not believed? and how shall they believe in Him of whom they have not heard? and how shall they hear without a preacher?' . . . If the heathen could be saved without the Gospel, why waste time, money and lives in taking it to them?

"This terrible unbelief and sentimental ignorance is far more common and deadly than most true Christians realize. Whoever heard of a soul-winner, a great giver

116

of money, or a prayer-warrior for missions who believed that the heathen could be saved without the Gospel?"

The heathen themselves have a fixed realization that they are lost, even while alive. They seem to realize that there is no true or sure hope in their pagan religions and empty ceremonies, though punctiliously performed. They universally fear and shun death even though their physical lives are frequently nothing more than an endless routine of misery; suffering, and woe. And the only reason they fear death is that they realize they are without hope for the future. *They know they are lost.* Anyone who has carefully observed heathen people over a period of time at close range realizes this.

Are there not multitudes of souls in that dismal world of suffering and despair below, from the benighted heathen lands, who are pleading and calling for someone to go to their people with the Gospel? Who that is familiar with scriptural truth could doubt it? Then can you say, Christian young man, that you have never heard a missionary call?

And let us not overlook this startling fact: That call from the dead can only be responded to by the living! Lazarus, or no one else, could be sent back from Paradise to witness to the rich man's lost living loved ones. (Fortunately, *His* brethren *had* the Scriptures—*the heathen have no light unto salvation*). I doubt not that there are souls in Paradise who would willingly come back to earth as missionaries to souls in darkness and sin, but it is not in their lot or power to do so. We alone, who know Christ and are living yet upon this earth, can be messengers and witnesses to His Gospel and saving grace. What a solemn responsibility! And also what a holy privilege. O, how can we fail to hear the call of the lost that rises from the hearts of the living and dead, and to do all that in us is to get the message of Christ to those who may still be snatched as brands out of the fire?

4

Then there is also, definitely, *The Call That Comes from the Inward Regions of the Heart.*

By this we mean *that personal and specific call of the Holy Spirit,* making known God's will and plan clearly and plainly to the inner consciousness. This is what all earnest young Christians are concerned about. Since we have discussed this very matter at some length in Chapter XI we will not repeat the same things here. We shall rather resort, presently, to what we trust will be some helpful illustrations. If one has truthfully taken the *preliminary steps* marked out by Paul in Romans 12:1, 2, dealt with in our Chapters VII, VIII and IX, the Holy Spirit will not fail to make God's personal plan known to the individual life. To suggest or think otherwise would be, in reality, an insult to the Spirit, for certainly one of His chief functions is to instruct and guide the Christians. For that very purpose He indwells us.

But here is a very important fact to remember: That Inward Call is not likely to be heard by anyone unless, and until, he has heeded the outward calls. We are quite persuaded that this is true. Unless you have prayerfully heeded the call of the needy fields, the call of Christ in the written Scriptures, the call of the doomed souls in hell, it is not likely you will ever hear the still, small voice of the Spirit, saying *"This is the way."* Make no mistake about this, Christian. If you turn a deaf

118

ear to these other three calls, the Holy Spirit will not issue the fourth and final to your heart. But if you have earnestly and prayerfully heard, heeded, and considered the outward calls, then, when the time comes, you will surely hear that personal, inward call.

Recently there was a severe fire near our Mission Home in Kansas City. An ancient apartment dwelling went up into a furious conflagration in a matter of minutes, and seven people were burned to death in the inferno. Fire apparatus came from all directions. Firemen poured off the trucks and went into quick and systematic action. Desperate and heroic efforts were put forth to save the trapped persons—and numbers were saved. But the striking thing during their efforts was the way all the firemen worked on specific instruction from the Fire Chief. Each man was detached to his own particular job: some handled the water hose, some erected giant rescue ladders, some ascended those ladders and rescued frantic men and women from blazing windows, some broke in doors and battered partitions, some applied emergency aid to the injured, others again stayed by the trucks and saw that the engines and pumps kept going to supply water to the blaze. The chief's orders were clear and crisp. No one was left in doubt as to his specific task. No one was left out of a job to do. And as they all worked together in compliance with the chief's orders, the work they did was little short of miraculous.

The Holy Spirit is our Chief. He is the one who must direct this great rescue work, and assign the individual workers to their task. And He will be no less anxious or definite about it than that fire chief was. But here is an important thing to remember: The reason those firemen received their instruction that fateful morning was that they had long before that time heeded the general call that had been issued for men to join the firemen's crew. The city had issued a call for help on the Fire Department; doubtless the importance of the work had been pointed out, the imperative need, the advantages, etc. It was a *general call,* but those men had heeded it. They had volunteered for the service. They were then put into training in the art of fire-fighting and rescue work. Now, when the time comes for actual work, they are at hand, ready, fitted, prepared to receive and carry out the Chief's instructions—all because they had heeded the general call earlier. So with the Christian! If he will not give earnest heed to the outward calls first, he will never receive a specific call to a given field at any time.

Dr. Harold R. Cook, whom we have previously quoted says, "No one should go to any mission field without a sense of call if he expects to enjoy God's blessing on his ministry. But to look or wait for an experience which at best is quite unusual is to open the way for disappointment and frustration. There are two aspects of the missionary call, one general and one particular, and the first is fundamental to the second.

"The general missionary call is synonymous with the Great Commission. It is expressed in various ways: 'Go ye therefore and teach all nations;' 'Go ye into all the world and preach the Gospel;' 'As my Father hath sent me, even so send I you;' 'Ye shall be witnesses unto Me . . . unto the uttermost part of the earth;' but the message is the same. It is the call of Christ to those who follow Him to go out and witness for Him everywhere.

"This call is general because it includes all Christians as prospective missionaries, and all unbelievers as the missionary field. It is not a question of home missions or foreign missions, of city missions or frontier missions. This is a call to be Christ's ambassadors to lost sinners without regard to where they may be found.

"There is no use trying to talk about a special call to the foreign mission field until you have heard and understood this general missionary call. It has been well said that a trip across the ocean does not make a missionary; neither does staying at home keep a man from being a missionary.

"Just as the general call to salvation is enough when the sinner hears it and realizes that it is meant for him, so the general call to witness for Christ is enough when the believer hears it and realizes that it is addressed to him. But to make it effectual, he too must say, 'Here am I, Lord, send me!' When God calls, and man responds, then the divine call is complete."

When the call of the fields, the call of Christ, the call of lost souls, sinks deeply into your soul in such a way that you cannot be indifferent, and still you are uncertain as to just where the Lord would have you labor, or just what type of work He would have you do, do like those men on the fire department. Join the force of volunteers for the work, go into training and get yourself fitted, and when the time comes to know your specific place the Holy Spirit will reveal it. Whatever you do for God, you need to know His Word. To know the Word you need to study. To study effectually you need to enter an institution for this purpose and engage in studying in a systematic way. If the general call to missions is touching your soul, launch out into training

121

so that when the Chief speaks, you will be ready; and then, whether it be at home or abroad, public or private ministry, you will be happy and blessed in doing His will.

15

SELF-CRUCIFIXION A NECESSARY PREREQUISITE

"I AM CRUCIFIED WITH CHRIST" (Gal. 2:20). "They that are Christ's have crucified the flesh" (Gal. 5:24). "Our old man is crucified with Him" (Rom. 6:6). "Likewise reckon ye also yourselves to be dead indeed unto sin" (Rom. 6:11).

Enough has been said thus far to convey to the sanctified, thinking mind that attainment of the knowledge of God's perfect will demands self-crucifixion. The natural man, the old self nature, is utterly depraved and beyond hope of any true spiritual capability or attainment, *permanently so*. It cannot be improved or cultivated into any spiritual capacity or ability. God cannot fellowship with depravity or communicate with it, or to it; He requires death for the carnal nature of the natural man. When a soul accepts Christ as his Saviour and Lord the old self-life is placed upon the cross, and is never to reign in that soul again.

"Self-ism" is, in the last analysis, the very essence of sin. Dr. A. H. Strong defines sin as (1) A state; (2) A state of the *will;* (3) *A selfish* state of the will. If you will study and ponder this definition you will see how truthful it is, and how full of meaning. The Bible views sin as the supreme choice of self, supreme love of self, supreme service to self. It is the putting of one's own selfish will, the *self-will,* in opposition to the holy will of God and the doing of what self desires instead of what God wills. To make our own happiness the ultimate aim of life is in itself sin, in its primary form.

"Sin is essentially egoism, or selfism, putting self in God's place," (Samuel Harris). It has four principal characteristics or manifestations; (1) Self-sufficiency, instead of faith in God; (2) Self-will, instead of submission to God; (3) Self-seeking, instead of honoring God; (4) Self-righteousness instead of contrition and humility before God. All the different forms of sin can be seen to have their roots in selfishness. Sensuality is selfishness in the form of inordinate appetites. Avarice, ambition, and pride are selfishness in the form of personal esteem. Falsehood and malice are selfishness in the form of personal justification and vengeance. Instead of making God the center of the life and unconditionally surrendering to Him, sin causes the heart to be turned against Him and makes our own interests the supreme motive and rule of our existence.

Let us give our attention now to a consideration of this vital and important matter of self-crucifixion. In order to do that properly we must consider crucifixion itself, for surely there is significance in the fact that the death prescribed for the self-nature in the Word of God is described by this awful figure.

1

Crucifixion Is an Unnatural Death. It cannot be stated too emphatically that the flesh, the old sinful

124

nature, *will never die a natural death.* It will never die of old age, but rather increases in vigor with the passing of time, so that an old person who has not been wrought upon by the Spirit of God will be much more confirmed in his natural tendencies and propensities, and far more unrelenting in them, than would have been the case in earlier years of life. This accounts for the fact that the majority of the people who are saved were saved in their teens.

Not only is it true that self will not die a natural death, but it actually resists death—is determined not to die. This is clearly evident. *Self will not die, it must be put to death.* This must be done by violence and force, as in the case of crucifixion. How violently and forcefully the Holy Spirit apprehended the "Old" Saul on the road to Damascus, and nailed him to Christ's cross! It was more than likely this incident that the apostle had in mind when he wrote, "I have been crucified with Christ." The old man will not die in any of us unless we enter into the same experience with Paul and are "crucified with Christ."

2

In the second place it must be recalled that *Crucifixion Is a Criminal's Death.* It was a death of ignominy and judgment, and was never inflicted upon an innocent or law-abiding citizen. It was not for the righteous, but for the unrighteous, the bad man, the outlaw. Now our natural man is all this and more. He is an outlaw in every sense of the word, having utterly broken and defied the just and holy law of God, in every form in which it has been revealed; he is a guilty criminal, *a confirmed rebel*. That is the reason God demands his crucifixion.

May God give us the grace to cry out against our flesh, as wicked men once cried out against our Saviour, "Let him be crucified!" Let us show no mercy, no compassion, no tolerance to the old sinful self, even though it loudly cries out for consideration. Justice demands death; a life in the knowledge of God's will and in obedience to God's will demands it; *self-pity* is giving ear to the voice of the evil one. Bear in mind that there is nothing good in self, only sin and iniquity, and thus secure it to that cross upon which the Son of God was counted as sin for us!

3

Again, *Crucifixion Is a Painful Death*. It is one of the most terrible deaths that cruel men could invent. Its agonies cannot be fully realized unless actually endured.

Oh, the pains of crucifying self! The old man "dies hard", and the pangs of his death are sometimes most excruciating. But we must not relent. As there cannot be such a thing as painless crucifixion, so there cannot be the crucifying of the flesh, with its affections and lusts, apart from "pain." If there are no pains in a man's soul it is a sign that self is not on the cross, and no spiritual progress is being made. But when the pains are the sharpest and most vicious, we must beware lest we give in to the pleadings of self for leniency; we must follow in the steps of Paul, and others who have more recently joined his train, as Bunyan, Brainerd, Judson, Carey, Taylor, etc.

The more a crucified man resists his inevitable death,

the more intense will be the suffering. Every move, every effort toward release adds to his torture. The best thing for a victim of crucifixion to do was to resign himself to his inevitable death, and remain as still and quiet as possible. Oh, that the old nature in us would but quietly resign itself to death! How much spiritual pain we would be spared. How many times of weeping before the Lord in deep remorse, how many seasons of inward agony, could be spared us. But, whether pain or no, self must be kept on the cross in the place of death, *and it must die.*

4

Lastly, *Crucifixion Is a Slow Death.* This fact holds the secret of the saint's most vital experience. Paul declares in Romans 6:6 that we have been crucified with Christ, and later in the chapter (esp. v. 11) he says, "Likewise (i.e. accordingly) *reckon ye also* yourselves to be dead . . . " Here is the truth in a nutshell: the old man is crucified but not dead yet.

A man may be crucified and live three days or more, and during that time he may speak, revile, rage, sneer, beg, and demand. The "old man" does the same in the believer, though he was certainly crucified with Christ. Our old self does not die at once but lives on, speaking, reviling, pleading and demanding, and will indeed continue to do so until our Lord in His own time and way calls us out of this world.

But once a man was legally crucified his end was inevitable; he was *as good as dead,* knowing he must surely die though he might linger on the cross several days. Such a man may be described as *living, yet dying.* When the Romans crucified a man his execution was recorded on the day he was nailed to the cross, and not the day he actually died. You see he was "reckoned" (counted) dead.

If some say the teaching that the old nature lives on in the believer is one of bondage, it is because they have not understood this point aright. An illustration: If a certain people had been governed by a tyrant king; and then a revolution took place in which that tyrant were crucified, would his subjects be bound to obey his commands and raging while he was nailed to a cross, doomed to die? Certainly not. They would count him conquered, helpless, *as good as dead.* So the Christian, although still conscious of the life of the old fleshly nature, can and must reckon him dead and consequently, he will enjoy true victory and liberty in his soul.

The Old Tyrant may be living, but is not reigning in the child of God, and none of us are bound or obligated to do his bidding. By virtue of our relationship to Christ we can reckon ourselves dead indeed unto sin but alive unto God; we need not yield our members as instruments of sin in submission to self-desires, but may learn God's will and submit ourselves to it. This is the way of victory and joy.

Moody Press, a ministry of the Moody Bible Institute, is designed for education, evangelization and edification. If we may assist you in knowing more about Christ and the Christian life, please write us without obligation to: Moody Press, c/o MLM, Chicago, Illinois 60610.